COFFEE

And Cookies

With God

Volume 2

31 Devotions for December

Becky Alexander, June Foster, Bonita Y. McCoy,
Suzanne D. Nichols, Ginger Solomon,
Lisa Worthey Smith

Kerysso Press

KeryssoPress@blogspot.com for media kit

Authors; Becky Alexander, June Foster, Bonita Y. McCoy, Suzanne D. Nichols, Ginger Solomon, and Lisa Worthey Smith, all members of the North Alabama Word Weavers, part of Word Weavers International

Printed in the United States of America

First Printing: Sep 2021

REL012020   RELIGION / Christian Living / Devotional
REL034020   RELIGION / Holidays / Christmas & Advent

ISBN-13 978-1-7361603-3-6
ASIN-B09FZS1ZT3

Kerysso Press

Dedicated
to everyone who loves CHRISTmas.
We hope your December is filled
with Christ
and plenty of cookies.

COFFEE *and Cookies* With God

Table of Contents

December 1

Christmas Negotiations

Therefore, holy brothers and sisters,
who share in the heavenly calling,
fix your thoughts on Jesus,
whom we acknowledge as our apostle and high priest.
Hebrews 3:1 (NIV)

"Open presents! Open presents! Open presents!" Sadie chanted. My five-year-old granddaughter had waited patiently through the honey ham, green beans, pickled eggs, and Christmas cookies. She knew the time had come to rip the wrapping paper.

"Before we open presents, we're going to read the Christmas story from the Bible," I said.

"I have an idea," she replied. "You could read the story *while* we open presents."

I chuckled. "No, we're going to read it first."

Sadie pondered the situation for a moment and continued her attempt at negotiations. "Well, how about you read just *half* the story then?"

As a Christian, I wouldn't dream of celebrating Christmas without acknowledging Jesus' birth and the good news of great joy. I treasure the biblical accounts in Matthew and Luke—a manger in Bethlehem, the shepherds, a multitude of angels, and wise men from the East. Candlelight services light my soul, and Christmas carols lift my heart.

I wonder, though … have I tried to honor the Savior's arrival *while* participating too much in the secular side of the season?

The world's version of Christmas attracts me with pretty packages and holiday parties, bright-colored lights and Black Friday sales, mischievous elves and roasting chestnuts. With little effort, festive events fill the days, pulling my mind toward the fun and glitter of December. Avoiding all the hype takes real intentionality.

I also wonder … do I sometimes "read just *half* the story," as Sadie suggested, to alleviate my busy schedule?

Hebrews 3:1 calls for me to fix my thoughts on Jesus. Offering an occasional, quick glance isn't good enough. I need a steady gaze amidst the bustle of life, an unbroken stare with eyes wide open in expectancy. That kind of focus leaves no room for cutting corners. Jesus has done so much for me. He deserves my best, my complete attention, the whole story.

Thanks to Sadie, I'm re-evaluating my December calendar. A few non-essentials are being erased, such as a gift exchange at work and a monthly friends' lunch. Several items of heavenly importance are being protected in red ink—my morning devotionals and bedtime prayers on my knees. I'm standing my ground about reading the story of Jesus first, and it must be read in full, from the beginning until the end.

No compromises.

No negotiations.

Dear Jesus of the Christmas Story,

Today, my thoughts are fixed on You. My gaze is unwavering, and my eyes are open wide.

Thank You for leaving a throne in glory to be born on Earth and placed in a humble manger. I am grateful every day for Your sacrifice, love, and gift of salvation.

In Your name I pray, amen.

Becky Alexander

Sadie Snaps recipe, page 152

My thoughts

Swaddling Clothes

And she brought forth her firstborn son,
and wrapped Him in swaddling clothes, and laid Him in a manger;
because there was no room for them in the inn.
Luke 2:7 (KJV)

I watched my daughter lay her newborn daughter across a folded cotton blanket. In three or four well-executed movements, she snugged the baby's arms close to her body and wrapped her into what resembled a cocoon, allowing only her head to move freely.

Baby swaddling has regained popularity during the past several years. Pediatricians, hospital nurseries, and new mothers have rediscovered the soothing effects nighttime swaddling brings to newborns, and even to babies several months old.

As my daughter gently laid her sleeping infant into the bassinette, I envisioned another mother kneeling beside a manger to place the newborn baby Jesus onto a cushion of cattle feed. In a shelter meant for animals, God provided safety, privacy, and comfort for this child—His Son—and Mary trusted His every move.

When an angel of the Lord appeared to shepherds watching over their sheep in the fields outside Bethlehem, the messenger gave only brief clues for finding the newborn Savior—*And this shall be a sign unto you: Ye shall find the babe wrapped in swaddling clothes, lying in a manger.*

The shepherds immediately went in search of the child. But a deeper examination of Hebrew tradition reveals they may have known exactly where to look.

If these shepherds were of the special group trained to care for the lambs meant for Passover and Temple sacrifices, they realized the significance of the angel's clues.

When ewes were ready to give birth, they were moved to special birthing caves kept ritually pure for that purpose. Lambs born for sacrifice were to be without blemish. Many scholars believe the shepherds swaddled the wobbly newborns to protect them against injury and ensure their perfection.

The angel's clues also matched the proclamation, *Today in the town of David, a Savior has been born to you; He is Christ the Lord.* I believe the shepherds recognized the fulfillment of prophecy because they understood the symbolism in the circumstances. And so, directed by the angel's brief instructions, they set out in search of what they envisioned: the promised Messiah, newly-born and swaddled as a perfect lamb, cradled in a feed trough in a ceremonially pure cave, in the prophesied city of Bethlehem. And that is indeed what they found.

~~

My newborn granddaughter awoke in the early-morning hours, vocalizing her demands. I peeked into the room to see if the new mom needed my help only to find her laughing at her baby girl whose arms now rested above her downy head, free from the restraint of the blanket swaddle.

I thought again of Mary. As she gazed at the perfection of her newborn, I wondered if she imagined how His arms—somewhat restricted by swaddling clothes in those moments—would later reach out to heal, comfort, and redeem the world.

Oh God of Promise,

From Genesis to Revelation, we trace the crimson thread of Your salvation plan. I marvel at how, for those who seek after truth, You have clearly revealed Your marvelous gift. As did the shepherds, I respond to the angel's good news of great joy and I come to worship Him—Christ the Lord, Lamb of God, heaven's perfect sacrifice.

In the saving name of Jesus, I pray. Amen.

Suzanne D. Nichols

My thoughts

December 3

What's in a Name?

... and his name shall be called
Wonderful Counselor, Mighty God,
Everlasting Father, Prince of Peace.
Isaiah 9:6 (ESV)

Tigers die and leave their skins;
people die and leave their names. ~Japanese Proverb

If I listed the names of a few people—Ebenezer Scrooge, George Bailey, or Saint Nicholas—you would know immediately about whom I spoke. We associate that name with the actions of that person, whether real or fictional.

The Bible gives great importance to names, so much so that God changed people's names to fit with who He knew they would be. Abram and Sarai became Abraham and Sarah. Jacob was renamed Israel. And Simon became Peter.

Isaiah reveals several names of Jesus in the above verse. *Wonderful Counselor, Mighty God, Everlasting Father, Prince of Peace.*

Let's consider those names.

First, He's called *Wonderful Counselor*—someone who gives counsel, advises, or plans. The word "wonderful" implies that His counsel will lead to good things. Jeremiah 29:11 comes to mind. *For I know the plans I have for you, declares the LORD, plans for welfare and not for evil, to give you a future and a hope.*

Then, He's the *Mighty God*. The word "mighty" here means strong, brave, or powerful. A warrior. Have you thought of Him as a warrior God? I haven't. Though I should have.

Joshua 23:3 reads *and you have seen for yourselves everything the LORD your God did to all these nations on your account, because it was the **LORD your God who was fighting for you**.* [emphasis mine].

And since He is the *same yesterday, today, and forever* (Hebrews 13:8), He still fights for us today.

Everlasting Father. Never ending. A lot of us grew up without a godly father figure, but I know what I would want in a father. Someone who supports me, encourages me, helps me through the hard stuff, and holds me when the hard stuff gets to be too much. That's how I see God as my father. When I'm struggling, I see Him sitting in His heavenly rocking chair and holding out His arms to me to come rest a while.

And finally, the *Prince of Peace*. The One in charge. The heir. The word for "peace" here is *shalom*. But it doesn't just mean peace. It also means: completeness, safety, soundness of body, health, prosperity, contentment, and friendship with each other and with God in a covenant relationship.

God also knows our names and He calls to us. Isaiah 43:1 reads, *But now thus says the LORD, he who created you, O Jacob, he who formed you, O Israel: 'Fear not, for I have redeemed you; I have called you by name, you are mine.'* And again, in the New Testament, John 10:3 reads, *The sheep hear his voice, and he calls his own sheep by name and leads them out.*

Not only does He know our names, but He knows the minutest details about our daily lives, down to the number of hairs on our heads (Luke 12:7).

God,

Thank You that You are all things to all people and available whenever we need You. Your name encompasses all. Thank You for being our counselor, our protector, our comforter, and our provider. And thank You for calling us by name and knowing us intimately, down to the very hairs on our head.

In Jesus' name, amen.

Ginger Solomon

My thoughts

December 4

Pretty Packages

He has no stately form or majesty
That we would look at Him,
Nor an appearance that we would take pleasure in Him.
Isaiah 53:2b (NASB20)

After having to wait many years before God blessed us with a child, I celebrated every moment of our first Christmas with our son. In an effort to preserve the joy, I mixed flour and water into clay and patted it into two small discs. In one, I pressed one little hand and in the other, a foot, leaving the impressions in the clay patties. After they dried, I painted the background to highlight the imprints of his hands and feet, wrapped them in many layers of tissue, and secured them in a cardboard box.

I had admired—and saved—a page from a ladies' magazine demonstrating how to create an extravagant wrap using ordinary wrapping paper. Determined to add an expensive feel to my very inexpensive clay gift, I hunkered over my kitchen counter and marked one-eighth-inch segments on the back of the paper. I labored for some time, folding dozens of tiny pleats across the width of one section of the paper.

When I turned it over, the simple pattern had transformed into a spectacular design. With the pleated section centered over the flat box, I painstakingly wrapped the paper over every corner of the box, careful to maintain the narrow folds. I tied a wide red velvet ribbon across the top that held the folds in place and taped a piece of greenery with a miniature brass bell on the ribbon as a final embellishment.

Admiring the extravagant wrapping, I thought it grand enough for an expensive watch or piece of clothing, as I saw in the magazine. It only held a few pennies worth of flour and paint. Somehow, I felt that the pretty package increased the value of the gift because it matched the magazine image of perfection and opulence.

God interrupted my prideful moment and spoke gently to me through the verse above. He didn't come to impress me with His outward appearance. He came to leave His imprint on my heart. Likewise, the treasure of my gift would not be in the outward wrapping, but the impressions in the clay.

He formed the first man from the dust of the ground and breathed life into him. According to Scripture, He made us in His image—to look like Him—to an extent. Because His handprints are on us and His breath is inside us, we are precious. Our true beauty will never come from our clothing, our coloring, or our features, but from being made in the image of God.

It wasn't wrong to take delight in the presentation of the gift. In fact, the recipient enjoyed the special wrapping. However, I needed the reminder that the paper only served as a temporary covering that would be discarded. The clay impressions were the true gifts, as the imprint of God within us is the most valuable treasure of all.

Gracious Father,

Thank You for the loveliest gift of all, Your Son, Jesus. Forgive me when I focus too much on the temporary beauty of things or people. Refresh my vision to see You and Your beauty within them.

Keep my heart soft so that You can press Yourself into it today. Having Your imprint on every aspect of my life will be my most beautiful and enduring treasure.

In Jesus' name, amen.

Lisa Worthey Smith

Thumbprint Cookies recipe, page 156

My thoughts

Far from Home

Jesus was born in Bethlehem in Judea,
during the reign of King Herod.
About that time some wise men from eastern lands arrived in
Jerusalem, asking, 'Where is the newborn king of the Jews?
We saw his star as it rose, and we have come to worship him.'
Matthew 2:1-2 (NLT)

Christmas in a faraway land, have you ever experienced it? Being far from those you love and the traditions and events that make the holidays special for you can be difficult, and trying to learn a new way to celebrate the birth of the King can be even more problematic. That's what I experienced the first Christmas my husband and I were away from home.

The second year we were married, we accepted a job out of the country and moved to a small island in the Pacific. Getting home entailed a long plane ride to Hawaii and an even longer one to the mainland, so we could only make the trip once a year for vacation. The option of going home for Christmas didn't exist for us.

This was the first time I had been so far from home that I couldn't go and visit over the holidays.

Not only were we far from family, but the whole experience of celebrating the holidays in the tropics flowed counter to how we had celebrated in the States.

Of course, the hot weather during December was new for us, even being from the south. No chill in the air, no ugly Christmas sweaters, no roaring fires. Instead, we had Christmas T-shirts, scuba Santa, and lights wrapped around the palm trees.

The kids used their Christmas break to swim and build sandcastles. There was no arguing over which relatives to spend the season with or last-minute shopping. On the island, you started your Christmas shopping in October if you wanted to make sure you had something under the tree for that special someone.

And everyone still had Christmas trees, but they were shipped in by barge, a little brown and dry. Most folks had fake ones.

Yes, everything in our new home was so different. Though I loved it, I must admit I missed my family and all things that made it feel like Christmas.

However, the one thing that sticks out to me about that Christmas was the celebration I experienced with the children I taught on a neighboring island.

Close to Christmas, they threw a great party and invited us to participate. Everyone dressed in bright colorful clothes and wore leis made from the island flowers. We exchanged gifts, small tokens of appreciation.

And we sang! The children, the parents, and the teachers lifted their voices, singing praises to the newborn King. How different the carols sounded in a foreign tongue!

Like the wise men who traveled seeking the one and only King, I had traveled to a far country and found Him there among the people. We worshipped. We praised. We prayed, and the babe in the manger received the glory.

I'll never forget my first Christmas away from home. The wise men had left their country to seek the promised King. I'd left mine to seek opportunity, but what we both found was something more wonderful and magnificent than we ever could have imagined.

Dear Father,

You alone are worthy of our praise. Thank You for sending Your Son as a babe, fully God and fully man. No matter where we are this Christmas, teach us to worship You with our whole hearts like the children on the island. Let our songs ring out to You this holiday season, whether we are with family or far away, and may our songs bring You glory.

In Jesus' name, amen.

Bonita Y. McCoy

My thoughts

December 6

The Christmas of 2020

Today in the town of David a Savior has been born to you,
he is the Messiah, the Lord.
Luke 2:11 (NIV)

Excitement, parties, food, church services, and family have always filled Christmases past. Shopping for the right present was a highlight of the season. What should I buy for the person who literally had everything?

Hitting the malls or making a homemade gift was fun. Parties—how enjoyable to get out my china and linens I haven't seen for a year, my lovely serving dishes reserved only for the season. What about the Sunday School Christmas party our class always had in the church fellowship hall? Needless to say, the wide variety of tempting fare had always proved to be delicious.

The quiet, candle-lit Christmas Eve service was always a marvelous tradition. Listening to my favorite Christmas story from Luke further put me in the "spirit" though I think I enjoyed the twinkling lights and the anticipation of the next day as much.

There is absolutely nothing wrong with all these things—unless they replace the real meaning of Christmas. It's great to gather with family and friends for fellowship by a roaring fire, open presents under the Christmas tree, enjoy those cookies and candy I only make once a year. But all that should not consume my entire attention.

Something happened this last year to challenge the usual way we celebrated the holiday. Would it still seem like Christmas?

The Christmas of 2020, everything changed for my husband and me. The threat of the Covid-19 virus kept us at home. No parties at our house or at friends' houses. Only a Christmas Eve service online.

Presents involved merely gift cards to family and friends who were hunkered in their homes hundreds of miles away. More difficult than anything else, the possibility of a cancer diagnosis hung over my husband's head, and we had to carry that threat into the new year.

My message sounds daunting, but I'm not finished. This last year I discovered a greater degree of joy accompanied by peace in our home. When the glamour and glitz were stripped away, something more beautiful and precious remained—the Lord Jesus and what He means to us as Christians. At times I had to hold my breath and listen, but the serenity was there.

Surprisingly enough, this last Christmas was one of the best. None of the normal trappings, but something else prevailed. Without all the usual holiday activities, I was able to draw near to the One who really matters, the One whose birth is the reason we celebrate. God's

Word suddenly became enormously important. I became more grateful for a small turkey dinner for two, knowing those dinners wouldn't last forever. Minus the distractions, Jesus' birth, death, and resurrection on the cross became more vital than ever.

Someday, I will see Him face to face, and His presence will last forever. Mistletoe, making cookies, and rushing off to parties will be long forgotten. I will enjoy fellowship with friends and family members for all eternity in worship to Him. As I look back, this Christmas was a preview of an unimaginable life we will have one day.

Dear Lord,

Thank You for sending Your dear Son into our world. Help us to seek the true meaning of Christmas.

In Jesus' name, amen.

June Foster

My thoughts

December 7

The Chapel on Christmas Lane

The Lord is in his holy temple; let all the earth be silent before him.
Habakkuk 2:20 (NIV)

Chapels top my list of places to see during road trips. I explore their history and take pictures of their design. If by chance I discover an unlocked door, I step inside for a closer look. A friend told me to make a wish upon entering a chapel for the first time and it will come true. Though I don't believe in wishes, I do believe in prayers. So, I send one up from each location.

On a trip to Frankenmuth, Michigan, I prayed inside the Silent Night Memorial Chapel on Christmas Lane. Everything about it fascinated me ... the chapel name and its happy address ... white, octagonal walls and a gold star above a domed roof ... stained-glass windows proclaiming the Christmas message in vibrant colors.

The story behind the building intrigued me, too. In Oberndorf, Austria, the pastor of St. Nicholas Church, Joseph Mohr, penned a poem for the Christmas Eve service. He asked the choir director, Franz Gruber, to add music. The two men debuted the tune on December 24, 1818, accompanied only by a guitar because the church organ was down for repairs. Today, the original Silent Night Memorial Chapel sits on the site to commemorate the modest beginnings of the famous song.

Inspired by a visit to the Austrian chapel, Wally and Irene Bronner constructed the Michigan chapel on Christmas Lane, near their CHRISTmas Wonderland store. In 1992, they dedicated the beautiful replica as "thanksgiving to God for His multitude of blessings."

Delights awaited me along a walkway around the chapel's exterior. Evergreens and lampposts lined the path. The familiar melody of "Silent Night" floated among the trees. Festive signs displayed the beloved carol in more than three hundred languages! My spirit swelled, while I scanned the words in various tongues.

PORTUGUESE (Portugal)
Noite feliz, noite feliz. O Senhor, Deus de amor.
Pobrezinho nasceu em Belém. Eis na lapa Jesus, nosso Bem.
Dorme em paz, ó Jesus. Dorme em paz, ó Jesus.

SOUTH SOTHO (South Africa)
Bosiu bo kgutsitseng. Tsohle di phomotse.
Ke Maria yo hlobaetseng. Le Josefa ya tshepahalang.
Bosiu bo bottle.Bosiu bo bottle.

We've shared the story of Jesus' birth through the simple words of a quiet song for two centuries now. The humble lyrics have provided peace and hope to countless people over the years. This season, may we sing "Silent Night" with renewed focus, knowing its message has touched hearts across the continents.

Dear God of All the Earth,

We lift a gentle song of praise to You in English, Portuguese, South Sotho, and every language of the world. "Silent night, holy night. All is calm, all is bright. Round yon virgin, mother and child. Holy infant so tender and mild. Sleep in heavenly peace. Sleep in heavenly peace."

In Jesus' name we pray, amen.

Becky Alexander

Silent Night Delights recipe, page 154

If you look closely, you will see the Silent Night Chapel on the front cover of this book.

My thoughts

December 8

My Messiah

For to us a child is born, to us a son is given, and the government will be on his shoulders. And he will be called Wonderful Counselor, Mighty God, Everlasting Father, Prince of Peace.
Isaiah 9:6 (NIV)

The stirring instrumentals and powerful lyrics of Handel's *Messiah* filled the house as I placed the finishing touches on our beautiful ceramic Nativity. The heavenly angel, perched atop a mantel clock, looked down on the scene arranged across the cabinet in our foyer. All the figures, in their gilded clothing and painted expressions, focused on the central piece—the Christ-child in the manger.

"And His name shall be call-ed, Wonderful … Counselor … The Mighty God … The Everlasting Father … The Prince of Peace!" rang Handel's bold proclamation of the Messiah prophesied by Isaiah some seven-hundred years before His birth.

Seven-hundred years.

Such a long-awaited promise. Generation after generation relayed that promise, watching and waiting for His appearance.

I surveyed the Nativity scene and wondered, "What did each generation tell the next? How did they interpret Isaiah's prophetic titles for the child to be born as their Messiah?"

Perhaps, as the Wonderful Counselor, they envisioned a wise leader with great ability to guide His people. In their expectations of Him as the Mighty God, biblical history indicates they longed for a powerful warrior, victorious over their enemies.

They were certain an Everlasting Father would always care for them, always provide for His children. And they longed for an end to all worry and strife with their Messiah reigning as the Prince of Peace.

As strains of the *Messiah* played on, I gazed round the room from the Nativity, to the Christmas tree, and to the gifts beneath it. One of the most enjoyable aspects of the Christmas season is a sense of anticipation and eagerness for what is to come.

Still, a pang of uncertainty gripped me as I considered my surroundings and wondered how all this showiness, the parties, and the gifts, became our way of expressing the arrival of the long-awaited Savior. Does all this celebrate His titles, His attributes, or His purpose appropriately?

As the music continued, I bowed my head and whispered to *my* Messiah, *my* Savior, "Lord Jesus, as my Wonderful Counselor, You lead me with unmatched wisdom. As my Mighty God, You conquer sin and bring victory to my life. As my Everlasting Father, You are my ambassador to the throne of God. As my Prince of Peace, You comfort me with hope, love, and joy."

I lingered before the Nativity, allowing the words of my prayer to soak into my soul as the music drifted around me in that worshipful moment.

With a fresh awareness, I realized the scene needed one more element.

I hurried to collect the necessary art supplies and returned a short time later with a small, hand-lettered sign—Isaiah's prophetic declaration penned from Isaiah 9:6. I placed it next to the angel perched above the Nativity and then stood motionless before the scene as the music intensified, "And He shall reign forever and ever!"

O God of My Salvation,

You have provided for all my needs in Christ Jesus, my Messiah. May my Christmas celebrations express my daily worship of Him as King of kings and Lord of lords.

In the powerful name of Jesus, I pray. Amen.

Suzanne D. Nichols

Creche Cookies recipe, page 134

My thoughts

December 9

Most High

The angel said to her, ...
'He will be great and will be called the Son of the Most High.'
Luke 1:30, 32 (NASB20)

The day after Thanksgiving, my husband makes his annual trek to the attic to retrieve our best-yet, Christmas tree—a pre-lit nine-footer.

Our first Christmas as a married couple, several decades ago, we bought an inexpensive live cedar that filled the small den with fragrance, but its wimpy limbs could only support strands of tinsel and paper ornaments. It was good.

The following year I splurged on a blue spruce that was strong enough to hold the wooden decorations I added that year. We didn't dare add electric lights for fear of fire, but it was an improvement over the cedar.

In the following years, I added fancier decorations and invested in an artificial tree with limbs that resembled bottle brushes. Strong and safe from fire, I added long strands of blinking lights and thought it was perfect.

However, every few years a better version became available. When our bottle-brush tree grew nearly bald from packing and unpacking every year, we found a pre-lit tree on sale after Christmas. It looked like a real tree and was half-price, so we upgraded again, discarding the old for something better.

No matter the quality of tree, I always reserved the pinnacle of our tree for either a star or an angel. Neither one was the most important part of Christmas, but the tip-top of the tree always caused me to consider what Gabriel said about Jesus' name and His place— Son of the Most High—in the Greek, *hypsistos.* Angels reiterated the superlative the night Jesus was born, praising God with, *Glory to God in the highest.* Luke 2:14 (NASB20) Days before His crucifixion, when Jesus neared Jerusalem, the crowds recognized Him as, *Hosanna in the highest!* Matthew 21:9 (NASB20)

~

In our modern-day gift-giving season, advertisers entice us to update our wish lists and giving lists to include the best and newest version of everything. They promise if we buy their new version, it will be better than all those before it.

Of course, next year it will be outdated.

As a young girl, I remember receiving my first Barbie that had bendable legs. What an improvement from the stiff-legged dolls I had. In this electronic age, computers that astonish us this year, will be outdated within months.

It's true that we continue to improve the things we make, but God will always remain Most High. Not only is He Most High, He gave us a gift that will never be surpassed by any other. There will never be an improved Savior, nor will anything or anyone exceed the name or power of God Almighty and His Son, Jesus.

Dearest Father and Most High God,

Through Your Son, Jesus, I boldly approach Your throne in praise. There is no other who can compare to You. The highest place in my thoughts, my desires, my motives, my actions, and most certainly my praise is reserved for You.

I pray I will always seek You as the incomparable gift above all other gifts and be careful to share You with those I meet.

I pray this in the precious name of Jesus, Son of the Most High God, amen.

Lisa Worthey Smith

My thoughts

December 10

Two Christmas Ornaments

And there were shepherds living out in the fields nearby,
keeping watch over their flocks at night.
An angel of the Lord appeared to them, And the glory of the Lord
shone around them, and they were terrified.
But the angel said to them, "Do not be afraid.
I bring you good news that will cause great joy for all people."
Luke 2:8-10 (NIV)

I curled my feet under my legs in the comfortable living room chair. Our Christmas tree winked with lights of red, green, and gold. My favorite ornament caught my attention, and I sighed as I remembered the first Christmas we hung the special decoration there.

Our oldest daughter's green wreath constructed of colored pom poms and a red bow had grown tattered and faded over the decades. In the center, her image remained, a sweet nine-year-old child with a smile on her face. She created the ornament in Sunday School and proudly presented it to her dad and me years ago. Now she's a thirty-nine-year-old adult.

I stood and strolled to the tree. The delightful aroma of gingerbread cookies baking in the oven perfumed the air. I glided my fingers over the hand-painted frame of another ornament, this one made by our younger daughter. She'd pasted a picture of our family dog, Sam, who seemed like a son to my husband and me—a bittersweet memory now that Sam had gone to doggie Heaven.

It seemed like only yesterday, but now my little girls had grown up, and I couldn't do anything about it. Life marched on, changes came, and our children had left home. I sighed and ended my trip down memory lane.

Sitting once again in my chair, I picked up my Bible and turned to Luke chapter two. "Do not be afraid. I bring you good news that will cause great joy for all the people. Today in the town of David a Savior has been born …" I stopped and gazed at the orange flames dancing in the fireplace. I couldn't get past the word *Savior*. I repeated the word over and over, and each time it brought not only joy but a sensation of standing on firm ground. Jesus is an entity that never changes, never leaves home. He always abides with me.

The simple meaning thrilled my soul. Jesus left His home in Heaven to become restrained by time and space on earth. He arrived as a tiny baby yet His role as Savior never changed. He walked the earth for approximately 12,045 days. On one of those days, He taught his disciples to pray. On many others, He taught people how to live and love each other. And on one day, He made the supreme sacrifice giving his life for us all.

The reality of the message hit me square in the middle of my heart. One day we will see Jesus face to face. One day we'll live in His presence for all eternity. One day, a day will never end. Heaven and God's Kingdom don't change.

Hallelujah.

Though I think about my children who've grown up, my Savior Jesus never changes.

Dear Lord,

I thank You for the reality of Jesus Christ, our Savior. You sent Him to this earth for a specific purpose as an extension of Your love. Through Him and Him alone can we receive forgiveness of sins and join You someday in heaven.

In Jesus' name, amen.

June Foster

June's Gingerbread Cookies recipe, page 138

My thoughts

December 11

Gift of Hope

Put your hope in the LORD,
for with the LORD is unfailing love and ... full redemption.
Psalm 130:7 (NIV)

I breezed past the Christmas tree in my living room, almost upsetting one of its ornaments with the big, striped box I carried. Slow down, I told myself. With only two weeks remaining until Christmas, I was certainly emersed in the holiday hustle and bustle. Today, however, an unexpected task had my full attention.

I packed up a very old coat today. It's the same coat my Aunt Sarah wore in the 1950's while attending nursing school. The coat is knee-length now, but it was almost ankle-length then. That is, until the day my aunt got caught in the rain, and her mother—my grandmother—tried to dry it out over the floor furnace. Unfortunately, the heat scorched the lower portion of the beautiful cranberry-colored wool coat.

But, being an industrious woman, and one not easily defeated, my grandmother made a straight cut way above the hem, removing all the burned fabric. She re-hemmed the shortened length and fashioned a button-on hood from the salvaged scraps. Although slightly redesigned, the coat's value was preserved and its purpose renewed simply because my grandmother saw promise among the ruins.

The coat was more than twenty years old when my grandmother gave it to me as a young newlywed. I not only needed a coat then; I also needed to see, through her reassuring example, that I could put my mistakes in the past and make the best of each day's new experiences.

Cherished memories flooded my mind and I marveled at the significance this coat held for me. Its appeal stretched beyond classic lines, lovely color, and warm fabric. My grandmother's vision and determination gave it an intangible quality more lasting and more valuable than the coat alone. I realized it had a story to tell, and the theme of that story was hope.

So, today, I've packed it into a box. Not to store it away somewhere as a precious, untouchable keepsake but to let it go, to offer it a renewed purpose with a special young lady.

I heard her say she needed a coat, and I instantly knew I could fill that need.

Although she is almost twenty years my junior, it's not difficult for me to see myself in her. A newlywed as I once was, she is learning and growing, determined to find hope in the trenches of her circumstances. She is now a wiser young lady; one willing to let God redeem the remaining value of a life scorched by wrong decisions. She is courageously allowing Him the freedom to cut away the ruins and redesign her, trusting His hands to form a thing of beauty and purpose out of pain and loss.

Settling into my car with the big, striped box on the seat beside me, I whispered a prayer for this young lady—the recipient of this sorrow-turned-solution gift. As I prayed, I rejoiced over yet another realization: the story of this coat is very much the message of Christmas. For in our hopelessness, God provided redemption through His Son. This Redeemer has come to reclaim scorched and ruined lives, to restore beauty and purpose, to bring victory out of loss.

O God of Hope,

Take our ruin and sorrow. Restore us for Your glorious purpose. Make Your redemption story the theme of our lives.

I pray in the victorious name of Jesus, amen.

Suzanne D. Nichols

My thoughts

December 12

The Star of Bethlehem

Then Herod called for a private meeting with the wise men,
and he learned from them the time when the star first appeared.
Matthew 2:7 (NLT)

King Herod had been running his little section of the world unaware that anything spectacular was going on under his nose. Neither he nor his counselors had spotted the star in the east and no one had thought about the old prophecy of Micah for some time.

Then some unannounced visitors showed up from a distant land that had once invaded Judea and had afforded Herod the opportunity to seize the power he now held. Nervous about this band of travelers, he wanted to know why they'd come. What were these magi seeking?

Imagine his surprise when they told him of the birth of the King of the Jews. A babe, not much more than six miles away who would be the shepherd of God's people. Herod needed a plan and quick. He couldn't lose the power he held, and he wouldn't let this baby get in his way.

We all know how the story played out. Herod didn't bother to travel the six miles to Bethlehem. Instead, he asked the magi to report back when they had found the babe, so that he, too, could go and worship Him.

Whenever I read this part of the Christmas story, I want to call Herod what he is ... a phony baloney, a bad egg. If the Christmas story has a bad guy, Herod is it.

But wait ... as I examine his reluctance to seek the child, when I look at his request for the magi to do all the work, when I put the spotlight on his absolute lack of awareness of what God was doing around him, I can't help but wonder am I like Herod?

How often have I let other commitments or events get in my way of spending time seeking God and His Kingdom? When I put myself under the microscope, I must admit there are times I've been lazy in growing my relationship with the Lord. I've let other things creep in and shorten my time with Him or steal it altogether.

And what about letting my pastor or other church leaders do all the heavy lifting when it comes to my worship of the Lord? Do I take responsibility for showing gratitude and thankfulness to my Savior, or do I leave that for Sundays only?

None of us knows all that God is doing in or around us, but we should be aware that He is working, and working for our good. I can't count the times I've let my eyes settle on what is wrong and forgot to put my eyes on the Lord. Keeping our eyes on Him and seeking His thoughts on the issues we face will help us to be aware of what He is doing in our corner of the world.

This Christmas, I want to take a closer look at my relationship with the King of kings. Is it growing? Do I spend time with Him and seek to know Him better? It's not too late. Unlike Herod, my story can be changed for the better.

Dear Father,

Please forgive me when I let other things crowd out my time with You. Help me to always be willing to go the distance to find out more about who You are and keep me focused on what You are doing in this world, so I can be a part of spreading the hope we have in Jesus.

In Jesus' name, amen.

Bonita Y. McCoy

Nana's Christmas Cookies recipe, page 150

My thoughts

December 13

The Boy Without a Coat

And the crowds asked him, "What then should we do?"
In reply he said to them,
"Whoever has two coats must share with anyone who has none;
and whoever has food must do likewise."
Luke 3:10-11 (NRSV)

As the Alabama temperatures dropped in late November, the children who didn't have coats were easy to spot.

My daughter, Cassie, called one day from the elementary school where she taught. "Mom, lots of these kids are coming to school in T-shirts, without coats. A few even arrived wrapped in blankets. We've got to do something."

"I'm on it!" I said.

I shot an email to family and friends. "Can you help? Many kids at Cassie's school need coats. All sizes, boys and girls, used or new. Hats, gloves, and scarves too. Bring them to my house by December 7, and I'll get them to the school counselor for distribution. Thanks a million, and Merry Christmas."

Over the next two weeks, a pile of colorful coats and winter accessories grew in my guest room. Some people dropped off lightly worn jackets their kids had outgrown, and others gave new ones in a variety of sizes. I hunted for bargains at local thrift shops and used donated cash to make purchases in department stores and online. In the end, we were able to gather coats for twenty-five children.

The school counselor teared up when I delivered the bags marked "girls" and "boys" to her office. She knew the depth of need more than anyone. "Thank you, thank you, thank you. This will help our families so much," she said, giving me a huge hug.

The counselor scanned her student list, consulted with teachers, and then chose twenty-five recipients. Some very excited kids went home that afternoon with a special gift of warmth and love.

The following morning, the children jumped from school buses and out of cars with their jackets zipped and snapped, snug and toasty in the cold wind. But one of the boys arrived wearing just a short-sleeved shirt again. Surprised, the counselor pulled him aside and asked, "Where is your new coat?"

The boy looked at the floor and spoke softly. "I gave it to my little brother. He didn't have one."

My family, friends, and I gave out of our surplus. I have five coats, maybe more. That boy, out of his poverty, offered the only coat he owned. His selfless example stirred a question within me: How much more could I give? Or from the words of Luke 3:10, what then should I do?

God wants us to be sensitive to the needs of others and to share our possessions with them. May we never forget the boy without a coat, his love and sacrifice for his brother, his precious and generous heart. May his caring actions inspire us to give sacrificially, during the holiday season and throughout the new year.

Dear God of the Little Ones,

I desire a heart like that young boy's heart. Help me notice the people around me with needs and show me what I can share.

And, God, I send up an extra prayer today for the children of the world. Please keep them warm this winter and reveal Your great love to them.

In Jesus' name I pray, amen.

Becky Alexander

Butterscotch Squares-to-Share recipe, page 128

Editor's note: The 2021 Florida Tapestry Contest awarded first place to *The Boy Without a Coat* in the short non-fiction category.

My thoughts

December 14

Unexpected Miracles

Then said Mary unto the angel,
'How shall this be, seeing I know not a man?'
And the angel answered and said unto her,
'The Holy Ghost shall come upon thee,
and the power of the Highest shall overshadow thee:
therefore also that holy thing which shall be born of thee
shall be called the Son of God.
For with God nothing shall be impossible.'
Luke 1:34, 35, 37 (NASB20)

A message from heaven defined two families whose lives would have otherwise remained unchronicled in history. God sent an angel, who announced they would each bear a son, designed with a purpose, for His kingdom.

In human terms, it was impossible for either woman to conceive, so neither family expected a child at that point in their lives. Elizabeth and her husband, Zacharias, had prayed for children while they faithfully served the LORD through the years yet had reached old age without children. Mary and Joseph, had not yet married.

While Zacharias performed his priestly duties in the temple, an angel appeared and announced that God heard his prayer. His wife, Elizabeth, would bear a child. With doubt in his heart, he questioned how he could know for certain. Because of his unbelief, Zacharias could not speak until after his son was born.

When the angel, Gabriel, told Mary she would bear a son, Mary believed it would happen. She didn't understand how she, still a virgin, could bear a child. The heavenly messenger explained that this would be a holy child, born of the Holy Spirit—Jesus, the Son of God. When he told her about her aging cousin Elizabeth, already six months into her pregnancy, he added a reminder that "nothing will be impossible with God."

Because Mary knew Who would cause it to happen, she accepted it as truth, even while she could not understand how.

~

I'm guilty of a Zacharias complex—skeptical, at least when I look to my ability and leave God out of the equation. Perhaps that's why Zacharias doubted. Maybe he thought of his and his wife's human inability instead of looking to what God could do.

On the other hand, Mary recognized Gabriel as an angel sent from God and trusted all that he said. She asked how it would happen, not doubting that it would happen. She counted on the Lord to do what He said, no matter how impossible it seemed.

Neither couple expected the blessing of a child at that time. Yet, in God's sovereignty, He provided unexpected miracles that didn't depend on their human ability, only their faith in Him.

Dear Father, God of the Impossible,

Thank You for recording these miracles that remind us You are the same yesterday, today, and forever, and remain sovereign overall.

Forgive me when I look to my lack of ability instead of remembering that nothing is impossible with You. Help me to trust You to accomplish Your will in my life. May my faith never again be based on what I understand or on my strength but instead, may I always trust You.

In Jesus' name I pray, amen.

Lisa Worthey Smith

Baby in a Manger Cookies recipe, page 126

My thoughts

The Aroma of Christmas

Now thanks be to God who always leads us in triumph in Christ, and
through us diffuses the fragrance of His knowledge in every place.
2 Corinthians 2:14 (NKJ)

The aroma of roasted turkey and dressing, tangy cranberry sauce, and
sweet potatoes with marshmallows drifted from my kitchen. I strolled
into the living room to glimpse the live evergreen tree offering its
piney scent. Only last week my grandchildren had helped me to
decorate it with colorful lights, balls, and tinsel. Afterward, we made
hot, steaming cocoa and tried our hand at creating homemade caramel
candy rolled in chocolate sauce.

As if I'd had another cup of cocoa, warmth filled my insides. I
couldn't wait. Our whole family planned to gather later today for our
Christmas celebration.

My husband wandered into the living room behind me and
plopped into his favorite recliner. "Don't forget our yearly tradition
before the crowd arrives."

I offered him my widest smile. "How could I? Reading the Christmas story together is the heart of our celebration—the true meaning of why we celebrate Christmas."

"Honey," my husband winked, "before we start, could we enjoy some of those cookies you made? I can smell them in here." I laughed and piled a bunch of gingerbread men on a plate then returned to the living room. The aroma of cinnamon, nutmeg, ginger, and cloves beckoned every time. I set the plate on the side table along with two steaming cups of coffee then relaxed into the chair across from my husband's.

He opened his Bible to Luke, the second chapter. After he read the story of how Joseph and Mary traveled to Bethlehem to register for the census and then she gave birth to a son in the manger, he looked up. "To think, the Savior of the world, born in such humble circumstances."

I only nodded as the story provoked deep emotion. The rest described how angels brought the good news to a group of shepherds at nighttime. When my husband closed his Bible, I sat back, savoring the holiday aromas mingling in the air. "The story never gets old." My hubby smiled and took a bite of cookie. "Something else that doesn't get old—the wonderful scents at Christmas."

"Just wait until I put the pecan pies in the oven."

He opened his Bible again. "That reminds me of something. Did you know the Bible tells us about another kind of scent?"

"The Bible talks about something that smells?" I laughed.

He flipped a few pages and read. "Now thanks be to God who always leads us in triumph in Christ, and through us diffuses the fragrance of His knowledge in every place."

"Wow, so everything we know about Christ can be described as a lovely fragrance—one that we can share with the world." I laughed. "I wonder if we smell anything like gingerbread cookies?"

My husband smiled. "Could be, or perhaps like this earthy aroma of coffee."

Lord,

Thank You that we can be a sweet aroma, spreading the knowledge of You wherever we go. Allow me to be a worthy ambassador, my Lord and Savior.

In Jesus name, amen.

June Foster

Crescent Cookies recipe, page 136

My thoughts

December 16

In the Right Place

They hurried to the village and found Mary and Joseph.
And there was the baby, lying in the manger.
Luke 2:16 (NLT)

When we were newly married, my husband and I moved out of the country to a little island where he worked for a government contractor. Each year the company would send its employees off-island for three weeks of vacation.

At the end of our first year there, during the Thanksgiving season, we flew to visit family and friends we hadn't seen in what seemed like forever. We were excited to tell them all about our adventure and doubly excited to share about the baby we were expecting.

We had a great time celebrating with everyone and preparing for the anticipated new arrival. But when we returned to the island, my husband was handed a pink slip.

So, while five months pregnant, I helped my husband pack up our belongings and head back to the United States with no home, no car, and no job, afraid and unsure of what the future held.

During those first weeks of being back in the states, we stayed with friends. They were wonderful to have us, but it was hard with so much uncertainty. I did all the things an expectant mother who wanted everything to be settled does—I worried, and cried, and prayed.

I can only imagine the thoughts that Mary must have had when she learned that she and Joseph would need to travel to Bethlehem for the census. So close to her due date, how she must've longed to stay at home where she had everything and everyone she needed to help her welcome the new arrival.

But God's plan is always perfect. Mary and Joseph's trip to Bethlehem fulfilled the prophesy foretold long ago about the King of the Jews and His birth. The meager manger transformed into the site of a miracle. The promised Messiah arrived without crowns or robes but surrounded by the common things of a stable. Displaced but in the right place.

Mary and Joseph had no guarantees other than God's promises and the certainty of His goodness. That's what I clung to as well, and God did not disappoint.

By the end of January, everything had been sorted out. We had a roof over our heads, a used car in the driveway, and an income. God had watched over us every step of the way. And our little one showed up, maybe not to a home of our own, but to the right place.

This year as Christmas nears, remember someone who is displaced or in-between situations and give them a helping hand. As

God's Word says, *When you do it to one of the least of these my brothers and sisters, you were doing it to me. (NLT).*

Dear Father,

Thank you for always walking with us and never leaving us nor forsaking us. Please be with those in our world who need a little help and let us be your hands and your feet.

In Jesus' name, amen.

Bonita Y. McCoy

My thoughts

December 17

Finding Your Treasure

The kingdom of heaven is like treasure hidden in a field,
which a man found and covered up.
Then in his joy he goes and sells all that he has and buys that field.
Matthew 13:44 (ESV)

My family didn't have many traditions at Christmas time. We put up a tree and on Christmas morning, we opened presents. Sometimes, we visited family but not always.

I wanted more for my children, so I created my own traditions and borrowed some from my husband's family. Now that my children are grown, some of those traditions have changed and others have fallen away.

A couple of traditions that have remained since they were little are goody boxes—treats similar to what you'd find in a stocking—and our annual "treasure hunt."

My husband came up with the treasure hunt idea, for me. He'd leave little clues on old business cards that led me to a gift, usually a special candy.

I modified his idea and used it for our children for Christmas. Even as adults, they still ask for a treasure hunt.

Each year, I spend an hour or more creating clues and writing them down on cards. Three to four per child times seven children.

For example, the clue to find the next card in the pasta could be as simple as "flour, egg, and water make this tasty food." Most of them are not that easy anymore. The struggle becomes making them hard enough to be a challenge but not so hard my kids become frustrated.

Their joy comes when they find the treasure. My joy comes in watching them wander our home, searching for the answer to the next clue and seeing how they work together.

I think our Father likes a good treasure hunt too. But His treasure is more precious than anything I could give.

To help in our search, He's given us the Bible. The Old Testament provides us with myriads of clues, while the New Testament furnishes a road map and a guide.

He understands that life is hard, and our experiences sometimes overshadow the truth. But just like when my children get frustrated with a clue and they come to me for help, we can go to Him. His purpose is not to keep us from the treasure. He wants us to find it. He wants us to find Him. But He also wants us to apply a little effort to discover the gift He freely offers.

Finding the treasure is all the sweeter and more appreciated if we have to expend a little energy to discover it.

In the verse above, the man found the treasure hidden in a field. Jesus doesn't specify what the treasure was, but to the man, it was valuable enough to return to his home, sell all that he owned so he could buy the field.

He had to do something to acquire his treasure. Selling his items didn't happen in five minutes or five hours. It took time and effort to accumulate enough money to buy the field.

Also notice, finding this treasure filled him with joy.

That's what finding true treasure will give us.

Dear Father,

Sometimes we work hard to accumulate things, but they don't give us the joy that only You can provide. Help us to seek Your treasure, the true treasure.

In Jesus' name, amen.

Ginger Solomon

My thoughts

December 18

The Dreaded Family Christmas Celebration

Therefore, as God's chosen people,
holy and dearly loved, clothe yourselves with
compassion, kindness, humility, gentleness and patience.
Colossians 3:12 (NIV)

Deck the halls and jingle the bells. It's time for the dreaded family Christmas celebration.

Your twin uncles, Grady and Garth, will be highly obnoxious, as usual. Cousin Caroline's five kids will run through the house unmonitored, knocking over at least two cups of coffee. Grandpa Lou will tell a dramatic story of outrunning a black bear, a tale you've heard eighty-two times before. And your mother-in-law is sure to criticize your technique for carving the ham. Just thinking about it twists your stomach into the shape of a beautiful Christmas bow.

Family gatherings can bring both blessings and stresses to our holiday season. We love our Uncle Gradys and Uncle Garths and wouldn't want to spend a Christmas without them. So, how do we make the experience better for everyone? Perhaps, we can be a thermostat instead of a thermometer.

A thermometer reacts to the temperature in the room. It assesses the situation and records the temperature. If it's sixty-eight degrees, the thermometer says sixty-eight. What happens in the room controls the thermometer.

A thermostat, on the other hand, sets the temperature in the room. It assesses the situation and takes action to make a change when something isn't right. If it's sixty-eight degrees, and it's supposed to be seventy, the thermostat causes the heating unit to start. The thermostat controls what happens in the room.

When we arrive at our family Christmas celebrations, we can assess the situation. Is the temperature comfortable? What can we do to adjust it? Are the following godly virtues present?

- Compassion–As a father has compassion on his children, so the Lord has compassion on those who fear him. Psalm 103:13 (NIV)
- Kindness–Kind words are like honey—sweet to the soul and healthy for the body. Proverbs 16:24 (NLT)
- Humility–Do nothing out of selfish ambition or vain conceit. Rather, in humility value others above yourselves. Philippians 2:3 (NIV)
- Gentleness–A gentle answer deflects anger, but harsh words make tempers flare. Proverbs 15:1 (NLT)
- Patience–Be patient with each other, making allowance for each other's faults because of your love. Ephesians 4:2 (NLT)

This year, let's attend our family gatherings with a mindset of action rather than reaction—equipped with compassion, kindness, and humility—prepared to demonstrate gentleness and patience. We can be a thermostat and change the temperature in the room to a merry level that honors Jesus.

Dear God of Compassion and Kindness,

Thank You for my wonderful, challenging family. Please bless our Christmas celebration with godly virtues. Help me recognize what I can do to adjust the temperature.

In Jesus' name I pray, amen.

Becky Alexander

Merry Tea Cakes recipe, page 146

My thoughts

December 19

The Gifts of the Wisemen

'For I know the plans I have for you,' says the Lord.
'They are plans for good and not for disaster,
to give you a future and a hope'
Jeremiah 29:11 (NLT).

God's provision rarely comes in the form I expect. It usually comes from a source I would've never thought of and in a way I could never have imagined.

For example, the year my aunt and I were praying about my future mate, I would have never expected God to use my older brother to confirm to me who it was I should marry. My brother had no idea that my aunt and I were praying over this matter, but once he met my now-husband, he told me out of the blue that I should marry him. And my brother, very wisely, was right.

In the Christmas story, we see another wonderful provision from God for the Messiah, Jesus. A group of astrologers or magi traveled from the east, probably from Arabia in search of the Jewish King. They saw his star in the sky announcing his birth, and followed it to worship him.

Assuming that a king would be born in a palace, they visited the courts of King Herod when they arrived in Jerusalem. Their news of the birth disturbed Herod, and he called the priests and religious teachers together to find out where this babe was to be born.

Herod passed this news on to the magi, and in return, asked them to come back with news of the child's whereabouts in Bethlehem so he too could go and worship. But he had no plans to worship the new king. Herod wanted to kill this threat to his throne and his power.

But God had a different plan.

God used the gifts of the magi, the gold, the frankincense, and the myrrh, to provide for the child and his parents as they fled from Herod into Egypt. God not only sent the wise men to honor and worship our Lord, but He sent them to provide for the practical needs that would arise as the Holy family made their way in a new country.

Oh, think how destitute the family would have been if God in his infinite wisdom had not stirred the hearts of the magi and sent them bearing their gifts.

God's provision. God's plan.

So, this Christmas season, I want to be open to God's unique ways of providing what is needed. It may not look like I think it will, and He may choose to provide in a way that isn't even on my radar. But when God provides, His provision won't be just for me. It will pour out, over onto others, causing all who see to praise the Lord.

Dear Father,

Thank You for the many times You have provided for me and my household. You have never left me to fend for myself when I've asked for Your help. You are a faithful Father who knows how to give good gifts.

Remind us that we need You in every aspect of our lives and that You know before we ask exactly what we need.

In Jesus' name, amen.

Bonita Y. McCoy

My thoughts

December 20

The Fruit of the Spirit at Christmas Time

But the fruit of the Spirit is love, joy, peace, patience, kindness,
goodness, faithfulness, gentleness and self-control.
Galatians 5:22 (NIV)

The book of Galatians mentions nine traits that Christians should exhibit in their lives. Paul defines these characteristics as fruit, and these qualities are demonstrated in our lives when the Holy Spirit indwells us. He goes on to say that those who belong to Jesus live by the Spirit.

Since it's that time again, I thought of the Bible characters in the Christmas story. Did any of these characters we read about in the second chapter of Luke display these characteristics in their lives?

Let's start with the shepherds who were living in the fields. These humble sheepherders were the first people to receive word about the birth of Jesus. An entire host of angels announced the good news to them at night when they guarded their flocks of sheep. They were filled with such joy, they rushed to Bethlehem to see baby Jesus, the long-awaited Messiah. After they saw Him, they were faithful to spread the word. *Joy and faithfulness.*

The wise men were foreigners who visited Jesus after his birth. They were faithful in coming to see the One whose star they'd seen in the east. They must've exercised great patience in making the long trip to Bethlehem. *Faithfulness and patience.*

Out of the many Christmas characters, Jesus' mother, Mary, probably demonstrated all the fruit. She showed peace when she discovered she was pregnant, patience in waiting nine months for her baby to be born, joy that God allowed her to birth the Savior, gentleness in her care for the baby's needs, faithfulness in her role as a parent, and her love for her Son. *Peace, patience, joy, gentleness, faithfulness, and love.*

The character of Joseph fascinated me as I thought about him as a man and not just the earthly father of the baby. When he first heard his betrothed was pregnant, he knew the child wasn't his. He showed his love for Mary by deciding to divorce her quietly instead of having her stoned. But after the angel of the Lord told him not to be afraid to take her as his wife, he proved faithful by providing for her and the Baby Jesus. And I'm sure he used a lot of patience and self-control in waiting until after the birth of the baby to consummate the marriage. *Love, faithfulness, patience, self-control.*

Let's stop and examine our own lives. What fruit can we claim as a result of Baby Jesus' birth? I'm the first to admit, without the Holy Spirit's power, I can display very few of these attributes. Thank God for his strength and guidance each day.

Merry Christmas all. I pray you're enjoying your tree, turkey dinner with family, carols, Christmas cookies, and in some places, snow. But here's a thought. A hundred years from now, what will matter most? Not the stockings hung by the chimney or gifts wrapped in colorful paper but God's gift to mankind, Jesus Christ.

Lord,

During the busyness of this Christmas season, please help me to keep my heart focused on the true meaning of Christmas. Allow me to exhibit love, joy, peace, forbearance, kindness, goodness, faithfulness, gentleness, and self-control to others this season and throughout my life.

In Jesus' name, amen.

June Foster

Lemon Cherry Cookies recipe, page 140

My thoughts

December 21

Starry Expectations

When they saw the star, they were overjoyed.
Matthew 2:10 (NIV)

News outlets announced the unusual event weeks prior to its occurrence. Intrigued, my husband and I made plans to see this rare appearance in the evening sky just before sunset on the twenty-first of December, 2020. Viewed with the naked eye, the orbits of Jupiter and Saturn would appear to converge, manifesting as one large, bright star. Journalists called it "The Christmas Star". The sighting would only be observable for a short time that evening, but even more noteworthy, such an event had not been witnessed in four hundred years.

Although we'd be traveling on December twenty-first to begin our Christmas visits with family, my husband and I were determined to see this once-in-our-lifetime alignment of these two planets.

At the first stop on our journey, we settled into our hotel room about an hour before sunset. As twilight softened the sky, we drew back the curtains on the south-facing window of our fourth-floor room and craned our necks toward the southwest horizon. Following

NASA's viewing instructions, we strained our eyes for any bright spot low in the sky.

Nothing. No stars, faint or bright, pierced the dusky skyline.

"That tree line is between us and the horizon," my husband said, tapping on the glass. "You'd think we'd have a clear view from four stories up."

Disappointment set in as we waited and watched. But no star appeared.

"We'd better get going to your mom's place," my husband sighed as he slowly drew the curtains across the darkened window.

We slipped into our vehicle against the cool December evening. As we made our way out of the parking lot, I noticed an oddly-shaped light in the sky. An airplane, I presumed. I lost sight of it as we turned onto the main road and headed toward the restaurant for the take-out we'd planned to share with my mother in her small apartment.

As we pulled into the restaurant parking lot, my husband received a notification on his phone about an unexpected package delivery. He quickly parked to review the message and search for someone back home to retrieve the package.

As he tended to those details, I gazed through the windshield into the cloudless sky.

"There's that strange light again," I whispered.

My husband glanced up, then focused again on his phone.

I watched the light for several minutes. "That can't be an airplane. It's not moving. Could it be the conjunction?"

My husband looked up again. "No. I don't think so. It's too high in the sky and not very bright," he concluded, turning again to his phone.

In the hotel room later that evening, I saw several photos of the conjunction posted to Facebook. Most captured the same scene I'd observed earlier—an oddly-shaped and not-so-bright light about sixty degrees above the horizon.

I excitedly showed my husband the photos. "It *was* the conjunction," I said. "We doubted what we saw because it wasn't what we'd expected."

What if the magi had been nonchalant in their study of the stars?

What if, even after careful study, they'd doubted the signs?

Thankfully, they were diligent, and they were certain. They believed the message of the stars and the prophets and it led them to the most wonderful discovery in the world—the Christ-child.

O God Who Guides,

Grant me the diligence of the magi that I may seek Your ways, believe Your promises, and lead others to the most wonderful discovery in the world. In the matchless name of Jesus, I pray. Amen.

Suzanne D. Nichols

My thoughts

December 22

The Branch

And this too fulfilled what the prophets have taught,
"The Savior will be a Nazarene."
Matthew 2:23 (The Voice Bible)

The Christmas tree stood seven and a half feet tall, too tall for me to place the angel in her usual spot. Even on my tiptoes, the top peak loomed just out of my reach. I smiled, remembering how over the years after all the other decorations had been placed on the tree that my husband would pick up one of the boys so they could place the angel in her perch at the top.

This year, because all the boys were grown, I worked alone to hang the decorations on the branches of the artificial tree. We'd given up on having a real tree long ago after one of the boys developed allergies. It seemed best at the time to find a good-looking fake one, and after we got one, we never went back.

I pulled and yanked on the limbs of the tree, trying to get the ornaments to stay where they were placed. The limbs had become bent with use and a few of the smaller sections had broken off. My husband

and I agreed it was time to start looking for a new one, but it was hard to let go of this one that had served us so well for nearly twenty years. A scripture from my morning's advent reading popped into my mind. *Out of the stump of David's family will grow a shoot—Yes, a new branch bearing fruit from the old root* ... Isaiah 11:1. The coming of Christ.

A new branch out of an old root. Jesus was the new branch. I had learned that Nazarene means tender, green, or living branch. What a wonderful way to describe the Savior, tender, and green, full of life. Yes, that's what Jesus was—the Living Branch.

I laughed at the irony. Here I was poking and pulling on a dead, fake tree, thinking about the One true Living Branch.

Maybe, I'm like the Jewish people of long ago, not wanting to give up the old tree of the law, wanting to hold on to what is familiar, even if it's not what's best.

I gave the tree a good once over. The green plastic sprigs twisted in every direction and the bare spots jumped out at me. The wires holding the thing together peeked out from under the green wrapped garland. This thing had seen better days. I shook my head.

No, with Jesus, the Living Branch, the new shoot, we have the gospel of grace. It is a gift from God not of ourselves. We can't earn it. We can only receive it. Jesus the Nazarene, the new shoot. The green, tender living branch that gives life.

I dragged the chair over to the tree and positioned the angel in her spot. Yep, this would be the last year to use this tree. The time had come for something new.

Dear Father,

Thank You for the living branch, Jesus, who died that I may have life. In Your wisdom, You have given me the greatest gifts of grace and freedom in Jesus to live as one who is forgiven.

May I live to please You and do Your will not just at Christmas but throughout the year.

In Jesus' name, amen.

Bonita Y. McCoy

Lynn's Christmas Molasses Crinkles recipe, page 142

My thoughts

December 23

A Familiar Ho Ho Ho

But the angel said to them, "Do not be afraid.
I bring you good news that will cause great joy for all the people.
Today in the town of David a Savior has been born to you;
he is the Messiah, the Lord."
Luke 2:10-11 (NIV)

For many, childhood memories of Christmas Eve include festive family dinners and piles of presents under colorful trees … sugar cookies with red and green sprinkles and wood crackling in the fireplace … popcorn to string and "Away in a Manger" at the piano. My memories, however, are filled with loud sirens and red fire trucks.

I lived in Madison Township, a small community in rural Ohio. Each Christmas Eve, volunteer firefighters gathered at the fire station at four o'clock in the afternoon to hook Santa's sleigh behind Uncle Kent's pickup truck. Following the annual route, they pulled Santa from one side of the township to the other. A caravan escorted him— two fire trucks in front, a fire truck and volunteer vehicles with portable flashing lights in back.

I'm not sure what would have happened if a fire had broken out in Madison Township on Christmas Eve.

Dad and Uncle Kent always participated in the tradition, against light objections from Mom for delaying our Selby family dinner. It was quite a thrill for us kids and a big part of Christmas Eve for the entire community. Kids from one to ninety-two stood in their doorways, straining their ears for the first hint of sirens, signaling Santa's approach.

Santa stopped in front of every house and talked to every child. For a sick child or an older person who couldn't get out in the cold, he climbed down from his sleigh and made a surprise house call. And, of course, the stop at our house was extra fun, as we had some special pull with Santa. I could never really put my finger on it, but his "ho ho ho" sounded a bit familiar to me.

When we grew old enough, all of us Selby kids got to ride in the fire trucks in Santa's caravan; we were his VIPs. Though disabled from several strokes, Grandma Maude even went with us one year, not too many seasons before she died.

As time passed, we moved away from that small town, and the "job" was handed to others. Yet, the Christmas Eve memories remain vivid to this day—loud, red, and wonderful! Thanks, Dad, for your love of Christmas … and your jolly laugh … which still sounds a lot like a guy in a red suit I recall from long ago.

Traditions tie together the years of our past and preserve them in beautiful memories of time spent with family and friends. This Christmas, as we celebrate the good news of great joy, which traditions should we carry on for the ones we love? What new ideas can we initiate to create happy holiday memories for them in the future?

Dear God of Christmas,

Jesus is our cause for celebration. Retelling the story of His birth is our first and most treasured tradition, one that we will continue with intentionality and boldness from December to December.

In His name we pray, amen.

Becky Alexander

Maude's Molasses Cookies recipe, page 144

My thoughts

Welcoming the Light to My Christmas Table

For God, who said, "Let light shine out of darkness,"
made His light shine in our hearts
to give us the light of the knowledge of the glory of God
in the face of Christ.
2 Corinthians 4:6 (NIV)

A pot of chicken stew simmered gently on the stove. Its cook and overseer—my husband—diligently tended the hearty, steaming goodness.

We were ready for Christmas Eve. Only one thing remained. Our guests had not arrived.

My brother was determined to continue the custom of making the long journey from his home in southern Louisiana, to East-Central Alabama to collect our mother and grandmother before finally reaching my home in North Alabama.

In the years since the tradition began, we lost our dear grandmother, my husband and I added a girl to the two boys in our family, and my brother married and gained a daughter. All those changes made it important to continue gathering this way at

Christmastime. We packed the short visit with gift exchanges, conversation over shared meals, making new memories, and reminiscing over old ones.

I listened for the sound of my brother's vehicle while I finished setting the table for the meal we would enjoy together as soon as the band of family travelers arrived. My mother would hand me a tin of freshly baked Tea Cakes as soon as she walked through the door. Close behind her, my sister-in-law would cross the threshold laden with boxes of homemade goodies.

With the place settings ready, I stepped back to survey the eclectic collection of candleholders stretching nearly the full length of the table. Red plaid ribbon intertwined the arrangement with slender, naturally-frosted cones from a white pine adding a rustic contrast.

I had assembled the assortment from various locations in my home. Some had been on regular display, others had been stored in a drawer, and the remainder had been boxed with other Christmas decorations.

Two were hefty and imposing. A variety ordinary. Several fanciful. Others delicate. Some were only a few years old. A number had been handed down from a previous generation or given as a gift of appreciation.

Simple. Charming. Certainly unconventional. But for me, the line of somewhat-matched but mostly contrasting holders represented the loved ones gathering in my home for Christmas. All of them reminded me of the uniqueness each of us added to the family.

As I pondered further, the entire arrangement transformed in my mind. The ribbon caressing each candle holder became symbolic of a shared faith in Jesus Christ woven into each of our lives through the generations. I saw the red candles in each holder as individual testimonies of that faith, meant to shine from lives as unique as the holders themselves.

I waited to light the candles until we'd all settled around the table. As each candle wick flamed to life, I shared my analogy and told my family how glad I was to have their presence and all it represented, shining on our reunion.

As we joined hands for a prayer before the meal, I was additionally grateful for Jesus, whose birth brought true light to the world and into the lives of those assembled around my Christmas table.

O God of Everlasting Light and Glory,

At Christmastime, and every day, may I turn toward Your Light and Your presence to then rise to reflect Your glory.

In the name of Jesus, the Light of the World, I pray. Amen.

Suzanne D. Nichols

Mother's Tea Cakes recipe, page 148

My thoughts

December 25

Faith in the Unknown

Joseph also went up from Galilee, from the city of Nazareth, to Judea,
to the city of David which is called Bethlehem,
because he was of the house and family of David,
in order to register along with Mary,
who was engaged to him, and was with child.
Luke 2:4,5 (NASB20)

Mary and Joseph hadn't planned to travel from Nazareth to Bethlehem, but the census required them to make the ninety-mile trip away from their home and family. Faith had already played an important part in their story, and this dangerous journey would require even more.

They likely endured cold rain during the day and freezing temperatures at night with only dried dates, bread, and cheese they'd brought with them for sustenance. Vicious predators including lions, bears, and thieves would have all lurked along the hilly roads to Bethlehem.

Both Mary and Joseph bore tremendous burdens. Mary, heavily pregnant and particularly vulnerable, would probably have been able to travel only about ten miles per day. Joseph knew the child she carried was from God but would have also known of the possible threats hidden along the route. Alone and vulnerable, their faith in God had to match whatever lay ahead in the unknown.

Maybe you've also been alone and vulnerable or prayed for loved ones far away and in danger. I have. When our son was deployed to the other side of the world, I survived—rather than celebrated—holidays without him while he served in a military "hot spot." Daily casualty reports reminded me of the hostility around him. I didn't doubt God's presence with my son or with me, nor did I doubt His love. Still, every phone call and knock at the door rattled my heart.

So, I prayed some of the most fervent prayers of my life and baked chocolate chip bar cookies. I dubbed them "deployment cookies"—a tangible reminder of my love and prayers. Moist enough to travel well, I packed them and mailed them to our son. Even though it took some time to reach his unit, according to reports I received from the Middle East, within hours after their arrival, only crumbs remained.

During that time, God reminded me to trust Him—more than I trusted any military training or equipment—with the life and safety of our son no matter how far away he was.

My care packages did nothing to improve his safety, but they reminded him of my love from a distance. I also needed the reminder that God and His love, was with us both, and His love was never distant.

God took Mary and Joseph out of their place of perceived safety and allowed them to be in a place of the unknown. They faced the cold, the hills, and the predators. God rewarded their faith with blessings and assurances that Mary pondered in her heart. No doubt they developed a deeper, more abiding trust in Him.

That's the kind of faith I want—the faith that assures me He will be with me and provide what I need when I walk whatever unfamiliar or dangerous path He asks me to take. May my doubt never be the fertile ground where fear can grow.

Dearest Father,

Grant the Blue Star Moms and military spouses an extra measure of peace during their lonely and uncertain holiday. Protect their loved ones in service. Anchor the Gold Star families with Your steadfast love as they face a holiday without their loved ones.

Help me focus on Your promises so that my faith will remain strong and I will be able to accomplish the tasks You have set before me, even in the unknown. Thank You for always remaining by my side.

I pray in Jesus' name, amen.

Lisa Worthey Smith

Chocolate Chip (*Deployment*) *Bar Cookies* recipe, page 132

My thoughts

December 26

Don't Be Afraid

Don't be afraid! Listen! I bring good news, news of great joy, news
that will affect all people everywhere. Today, in the city of David,
a Liberator has been born for you!
He is the promised Anointed One, the Supreme Authority!
You will know you have found Him when you see a baby,
wrapped in a blanket, lying in a feeding trough.
Luke 2:10-12 (The Voice Bible)

Imagine yourself going about your daily routine. You get the kids up
for school, feed them breakfast, and get them out the door. Your
spouse kisses you goodbye and heads off to his job. If you work
outside the home, you make it into the office, another day of the same
old grind. Or if you stay at home, you're busy planning dinner and
doing laundry.

Then out of nowhere a glowing heavenly being appears in front
of you, and the first words he speaks to you are the practical ones.
"Don't be afraid. Listen."

I don't know about you, but I'm not sure my finite mind could've
comprehended what was happening. An angel standing in front of me
wanting me to listen to his message. Me, Miss Ordinary.

Now think about those shepherds in the field that night long ago, simply doing what they did, encountering this miracle. This unexpected blazing angelic being beckoning them to stay calm and listen.

Then without hesitation, the angel announced something beyond comprehension, a Savior, a Liberator, the promised Anointed One has arrived. A message so astounding it would've been deemed difficult to believe by even the greatest experts of the time. A message so contradictory to what was expected it would've been laughed at by the learned and well-to-do.

The Savior of the world lies wrapped in a blanket in a feeding trough? Surely not. No way is the Supreme Authority tucked into a warm bed of hay in the place where the cows and horses would feed.

But the shepherds listened, watched, and beheld the glory of the Lord as the sky lit up with a multitude of the heavenly hosts. Angels everywhere.

One angel would've been enough to put me into a stupor. But seeing a countless array of brilliant beings singing praises to God and the practical advice to *fear not*, would've evaporated into thin air.

Not the shepherds. They heard the news and rejoiced at the tidings. Following the angel's directions, they searched for the child in the barns and stables of the town. And when they found Him, the Savior of the World, they praised God that everything had unfolded as the messenger had told them.

Now, I have good news for you. You don't need an angelic visit to receive the message given that day. Jesus is that baby tucked in the trough. He paid the price for all your sins. He is the message that you need to hear, and the wonderful news is that God sent that message just for you.

Whatever may be happening in your life, no matter how far you think you've gone, Jesus came to bring you certainty in your relationship with Father God. He came so that you would have everlasting life.

So, rejoice. Don't be afraid. A Savior has come, today.

Dear Father of Forgiveness,

I thank You that You sent your Son, Jesus, into the world and that You have made a way for all of us to know You. I confess I need a Savior. Traveling my own way, I get lost and afraid, terrified of what might be.

Thank You that no matter how far off the road we go, You are willing to forgive us and lead us back to Your path for us.

In Jesus' name, amen.

Bonita Y. McCoy

My thoughts

December 27

The Unexpected Christmas Gift

For even the Son of Man did not come to be served,

but to serve.

Mark10:45a (NIV)

My husband has come full circle. Born and raised in Cullman, Alabama, he's returned to his small hometown after serving our nation in the US Army and then traveling for a number of years in our RV. Of course, I've been right by his side. We love our new home and intend to settle there.

There's only one drawback. Most of our kids and grandkids live hundreds of miles away which limits our opportunity to spend the holidays with them. Rather than sitting at home drowning in self-pity and regret, we decided to give back to our community. But how?

The chance came when our church announced the need for Christmas Eve volunteers to deliver meals to shut-ins, elderly folks, and others with financial struggles. Many in our congregation have family members in the area who gather in each other's homes, so they would be less available. It was a win-win situation.

We piled the boxes of food into the trunk, organized our route, and set out for the neighborhoods. Knocking on doors and seeing the smiling faces was a Christmas gift we hadn't expected.

My favorite delivery was to a grandmother and her two grandchildren, a boy, five, and a girl, seven. She confessed her daughter had left the kids with no explanation, and she didn't know where the children's mother was. Since the grandmother was on Social Security, she didn't have much money for gifts.

The Caring Center our church runs provided two toys each for the children's Christmas. Her eyes shone when she received our basket filled with shampoo, toothpaste, hand lotion, and hand wash. The Center hadn't forgotten her, either. Not only receiving the gifts, but she and her grandchildren would also be able to enjoy the delivered meal. I slipped a children's Bible storybook in her hand and asked her to read the Christmas story to the grandchildren later.

As exciting as the stop at the grandmother's house had been, another visit also blessed us. An elderly couple who'd been married for sixty-five years lived in the small home. The husband was in a wheelchair, and the wife, crippled with arthritis, couldn't get around well. This precious couple attended our church at one time but could no longer leave the house. Along with their meal, we brought them a small holiday flower arrangement to decorate their table.

Our earthly family is far away this Christmas, but we still have another family—the family of God. *So, then you are no longer strangers and aliens, but you are fellow citizens with the saints and members of the household of God.* Ephesians 2:19 (NIV)

Just as we enjoy looking after and caring for our physical family, we want to serve our heavenly Father. And serve, we did. To see the joy on people's faces when we bring them a hot turkey dinner more than compensates for the lack of family. They are not only pleased that someone delivered a delicious meal but because someone thought about them.

Jesus came into the world to serve and not be served. It is a privilege to emulate Jesus by serving others.

Lord,

Thank You for the opportunity to serve others this Christmas. Thank You for the greatest gift of all, the birth of Your Son, Jesus Christ. Thank You for calling us Your own, that we might be a part of Your family.

In Jesus' name, amen.

June Foster

My thoughts

Back to Work

And the shepherds went back,
glorifying and praising God for all that they had heard and seen,
just as had been told them.
Luke 2:20 (NASB20)

In the darkness of that evening, heavenly messengers brought astounding news and an exclusive invitation to shepherds in a field. The long-awaited Savior had been born. Angels assured them they were welcome to visit Him in Bethlehem. The King of the Universe, born in flesh, welcomed these of lowly estate into His first earthly home.

They left their jobs and hurried to see the newborn King. No doubt they encountered glaring eyes when they entered the small town. Smelly shepherds rarely received invitations into town much less to any social gatherings. However, God sent messengers to request they come and see Jesus, the Savior.

The shepherds could have hidden among the shadows and left town without being noticed, but their excitement was greater than their fear of rejection or scorn. They eagerly shared with the people they encountered about the angels, and the baby, wrapped in swaddling clothes, just as the angels had told them.

After this exhilarating experience, they returned to work, forever changed.

Today, many employers provide their employees a day or more of vacation for Christmas. During the holiday season, we attend and host celebrations and freely speak "Merry Christmas" wishes to those we meet. We expand our normal menu to bake, indulge in special foods, and share these Christmas blessings with neighbors and family. Our home décor shifts to make room for trees and nativity scenes. Music and movies present the story of His miraculous birth during the weeks leading to Christmas.

Many gather with family and church friends, worshipping the Savior who not only became flesh and lived among us but who also took our sin penalty and bore it on the cross to pay our debt. He defeated sin and death once and for all to provide a means for us to be a part of His family for eternity.

The celebrations end and like the shepherds, we go back to work and transition back to our general "Hello" greetings. Most years, after the joy and excitement end, even if the results from the increased caloric intake do not, we go back to our regular routines with little mention of the tremendous gift of the Savior.

This Scripture leaves the possibility that the shepherds continued to tell of that night. As the days and weeks passed, I imagine they told it often among themselves. I tend to think they shared it with others they met when they herded their flock to green pastures in a new village.

Isn't that just like Jesus to invite the lowly shepherds to His presence? How wonderful that they did not waste the invitation, but spread the good news of the Savior's birth as they returned to work.

Father,

Thank You for this reminder that You welcome me into Your family and can use a simple person of little wealth or influence to share the good news.

As I return to my job, I pray You will nudge me to share the good news of Christmas in and out of the season. Help me recognize and be faithful to use opportunities in my job to glorify You in all my remaining days.

In Jesus' name, I pray, amen.

Lisa Worthey Smith

My thoughts

December 29

Lingering in the Awe

For my eyes have seen Your salvation,
which You have prepared in the sight of all people.
Luke 2:30-31 (NIV)

I returned from a quick trip to the grocery store to find my husband
seated on the couch, nibbling on Christmas cookies—Snickerdoodles,
to be precise. His glass of milk was within easy reach on a nearby side
table. I didn't question his choice of places in which to enjoy his sweet
treat. It was evident as soon as I walked into the house and heard
Christmas music resounding from all five speakers of our sound
system.

This man has a great appreciation for music. He plays the
trumpet, is learning guitar, and sings with a lovely bass voice. So, to
find him in the surround-sound sweet spot is never surprising.

Furthermore, to find him listening to Christmas music *today* was
completely understandable. Even though December twenty-fifth was
four days ago, it was yet another choice I didn't question. I'm well
aware that, from his point of view, the celebration of Christmas ends

too abruptly. He prefers to linger in the seasonal joys of special foods and decorations, and he especially enjoys the music.

I agree with his assertion that worshipful Christmas songs being sung for only a few short weeks does not allow enough time for appropriate attention to the birth of our Savior. This truth leads me to consider the responses of those who encountered the young Jesus.

From the shepherds at the manger to Simeon and Anna in the Jerusalem temple; and from the diligent magi to the teachers in the temple courts, each became filled with awe, captivated by every precious moment of the experience, reluctant to leave His presence.

The shepherds humbly investigated the angelic announcement, and then joyfully shared with others their discovery of the Christ-child. Simeon held the eight-day-old infant in his arms and declared the newly-consecrated baby to be the glory of Israel and a light for the Gentiles. Anna joined Simeon, giving testimony in agreement with his revelation. The magi bowed before Him in worship and presented Him with valuable gifts worthy of the promised Messiah. The teachers in the Jerusalem temple courts were amazed at the wisdom and understanding of the twelve-year-old Jesus as He conversed with them following the Passover celebrations.

These who personally witnessed His glory leave us the challenge to surround ourselves with a worshipful atmosphere at Christmastime and every day.

We have the privilege of knowing His story beyond His childhood, through His earthly ministry, to His sacrifice for our sins on a Roman cross, and His glorious triumph over death and hell. Through a personal relationship with Him as our own Savior-Redeemer, we possess a gift beyond the experiences of those who first encountered Him; we are living in His marvelous, continuing story.

I put away the groceries and joined my husband on the couch with a re-supply of Snickerdoodles. "We have plenty," I offered, projecting my voice above the rumbling rhythms and soaring melodies. "Enough to last through several more days of Christmas music," I added with a wink.

O Loving Father,

May I choose to linger in the presence of Jesus and remain in awe of the miraculous and marvelous gift of Emmanuel—God with us—at Christmastime and every day.

In the glorious name of Jesus, I pray. Amen.

Suzanne D. Nichols

Vikki's Old-Fashioned Snickerdoodles recipe, page 158

My thoughts

A Winter Marvel

Have you ever traveled to where snow is made? ...
Can you find your way to where lightning is launched,
or to the place from which the wind blows?
Who do you suppose ... charts the route of thunderstorms? ...
And who do you think is the father of rain and dew,
the mother of ice and frost?
You don't for a minute imagine these marvels of weather just happen,
do you?
Job 38:22-30 (THE MESSAGE)

The bedroom illuminated with a sudden, magnificent light, jolting me from deep sleep to disoriented consciousness. In an instant, the room became black again. I sat up in bed, in dark silence—except for the rattling of my windows. And then, boom! Something exploded outside, shaking the entire house.

I raced toward my son on the second floor. By the time I reached the bottom of the stairs, Isaac barreled down from the top. We yelled simultaneously, "What was that?"

I jerked open the front door, and we ran outside.

"Oh … my … goodness." I shivered in my pajamas.

"This feels eerie," Isaac whispered.

We stood in the middle of a winter wonderland. All was quiet. Five inches of beautiful white stuff coated everything and continued to fall from the sky. Our Alabama-where-it-never-snows mouths hung open. My secret order for a white Christmas had arrived—even if it was two weeks late!

"At first, I thought the light and blast might be the second coming of Jesus, but we're still here," I said.

"I thought the same thing!" Isaac exclaimed with a nervous laugh.

Clueless, we went inside to check for breaking news of an explosion in our area. Because the TV offered no answer, I opened social media. I figured someone else in our community surely saw that bright light and heard that loud boom. I was right.

One friend after another talked about their "thundersnow" experiences. Thundersnow. I'd never heard the word before. Apparently, the event was a rare weather phenomenon, and for Alabama, almost unheard of.

Excitement rushed through my body. I had just witnessed one of God's marvels of nature.

The Bible mentions God's control over the elements many times. In Mark 4:39, Jesus rebuked the wind, and it obeyed Him. Psalm 148:8 (NASB) reads: *Fire and hail, snow and clouds; Stormy wind, fulfilling*

His word. Elijah prayed for God to withhold rain from Israel, and it ceased for three and a half years. And in James 5:17-18 (NASB), Elijah asked God to end the drought, and *the sky poured rain.*

God orchestrates our weather from morning dew to evening frost, from gentle breeze to raging wind, from July sun to Christmas snow. We can watch the sky for daily displays of divine power. And when we least expect it, we may encounter a marvel.

Dear God of Marvels,

Your thunder shakes my windows and startles my spirit. Your glittering snow decorates my roof and delights my eyes. Your thundersnow—oh, Your thundersnow—fills my heart with praise for Your wondrous works.

In Jesus' name I pray, amen.

Becky Alexander

Winter Marvels recipe, page 160

Author's Note: This weather phenomenon occurred in Decatur, Alabama, on January 9, 2011. NASA reported: "It was a once-in-a-lifetime scene for anyone lucky enough to see it but especially enthralling to scientists seeking the keys to nature's unique displays of power."

My thoughts

December 31

Packing Away Jesus

No one lights a lamp and puts it away in a cellar
nor under a basket,
but on the lampstand,
so that those who enter may see the light.
Luke 11:33 (NASB20)

In the decorating community, the minimalism trend is growing in popularity. It encourages eliminating clutter and keeping no more than thirty books. I have no clue how to parse my book collection to such a small number. I am not a hoarder—no matter what my husband might tell you—but I admit I have a lot of stuff. Not all of it is essential to life, but it does bring me joy.

My Christmas decorations—far more than thirty boxes worth—bring me extraordinary joy. The day after Thanksgiving, I—meaning my husband—trek upstairs to retrieve stacks of boxes filled with Christmas decorations.

Because I've reduced my number of Christmas trees from two to one, I alternate my ornaments from year to year. Over several days, I unpack and place ornaments and decorations, considering the

COFFEE *and Cookies* With God

significance of their origin or meaning. Then I return the others to the attic.

While my exuberance for decorating has waned along with my physical abilities, my love for the decorations has not. Each ornament or decoration I unwrap represents an aspect of the miracle of Christmas and helps kindle the joy of the season. What might seem gaudy in July is welcome in December.

However, after Christmas, I wrap and pack away all the decorations. At least I used to.

Several years ago, I noticed a ceramic Christmas bell on top of my piano weeks after all the boxes returned to their attic shelves. My grandmother had painted it many years before with a green holly sprig dotted with red berries. It perched there over many holiday seasons, then spent the rest of the year in the attic.

When I discovered it, I could have wrapped it and shipped it upstairs to a box for the next ten months or so, but God nudged me to leave it. Why should I display Jesus only for Christmas and hide Him the rest of the year?

During that year, the holly bell prompted me to make music that honors him and that not only will Christmas celebrations return, so will He. The next year an angel stood watch on a countertop. One year, a wreath of jingly bells hung on a cabinet knob. This year, a tiny white porcelain angel sits in my kitchen.

Now I embrace this new tradition, purposely leaving a small Christmas decoration on display. Nothing as large as a tree that would catch the attention of a visitor, but something small that brings a sparkle of Christmas and the promise of His return to mind. I like allowing one decoration to receive more than its usual moment of glory and giving it the responsibility to display a little Christmas throughout the year.

Mostly I love the reminder that the joy of Christmas isn't confined to December.

Dear Heavenly Father,

Forgive me for so readily packing away all the reminders of Your miraculous birth in the years past.

Thank You for showing me how a little bit of Christmas all year long, can make a difference in my attitude, my goals, and my mission. Keep my heart receptive to ways I can share the joy of Your love and Your promise to return, throughout the coming year.

In the name of Jesus I pray, amen.

Lisa Worthey Smith

Candy Cane Cookies recipe, page 130

My thoughts

Cookie Recipes

Baby in a Manger Cookies

Gluten-free Peanut Butter Blossoms

½ cup gluten-free peanut butter

½ cup granulated sugar

½ cup firmly packed brown sugar

½ cup unsalted butter, softened

1 tsp. molasses

1 egg, room temperature

1 ¼ cups gluten-free all-purpose flour, (I use King Arthur all-purpose baking mix. If you use one without xanthan gum, you will need to add ¼ tsp. xanthan gum to the dry ingredients.)

¾ tsp. baking soda

½ tsp. baking powder

¼ (about) cup granulated sugar for rolling

36 chocolate drops – such as Hershey Kisses (Not all are gluten-free. Check label to confirm)

Preheat oven to 375°

Mix together the granulated sugar, brown sugar, butter, and peanut butter until creamy. Stir in the egg and molasses.

In a medium bowl whisk together the gluten-free flour baking soda and baking powder. Slowly add the flour mixture into the sugar and egg mixture until fully combined. The cookie dough will be like soft playdough.

Cover cookie dough and refrigerate for 30 minutes.

Place about ¼ cup of granulated sugar in a small bowl.

Scoop 1 Tbl. of dough and roll into a ball. (A cookie dough scoop makes the job easier.) Then roll it in the granulated sugar to cover. Place onto a parchment-lined baking sheet about 2 inches apart.

Bake for 10-12 minutes or until light brown on the edges.

While cookies are still hot out of the oven, lightly press a chocolate kiss in the center of each cookie.

Warning. The chocolate kiss will be soft for several minutes. Consider letting them cool before serving. If temptation doesn't allow for waiting, provide plenty of napkins.

Lisa Worthey Smith

Unexpected Miracles, page 53

Butterscotch Squares-to-Share

Butter to grease pan and hands

1 cup light corn syrup

1 cup white sugar

1 ½ cups peanut butter

6 cups crispy rice cereal

½ cup semisweet chocolate chips

½ cup butterscotch chips

¼ cup red decorating sugar, optional

Generously butter a 9x13-inch pan. Set aside.

In a large pot, mix together corn syrup, white sugar, and peanut butter. Cook over medium heat, stirring until peanut butter melts. Bring mixture to a boil. Remove from heat, and stir in crispy rice cereal.

Transfer mixture into the 9x13-inch pan. With your hands well buttered, pat it down.

In a medium saucepan, melt chocolate chips and butterscotch chips over medium-low heat until smooth. Spread on top of cereal mixture. Sprinkle with red decorating sugar, if desired.

When cool, cut into squares to share with others.

Becky Alexander

The Boy Without a Coat, page 49

Candy Cane Cookies

1 – 15.25 oz box of vanilla cake mix

(or chocolate)

2 eggs

1/4 cup of vegetable oil

1 tsp. peppermint extract

5 peppermint candy canes crushed

      (freeze, then use mallet)

Frosting

1 stick salted butter

2 drops peppermint extract

2 cups powdered sugar, sifted

Preheat oven to 350°

In a large bowl mix together cake mix, eggs, vegetable oil, and peppermint extract. Mix until smooth.

Line a baking sheet with parchment paper. Using a cookie scoop or a tablespoon, place mounded tablespoons of dough on baking sheet about 2 inches apart

Bake 8-10 minutes until tops are lightly golden brown. Remove from oven and transfer to a cooling rack.

Prepare frosting while they cool.

Melt butter and stir in enough powdered sugar to make a thick glaze. (Think consistency of pancake batter) When cookies are completely cool (if they are warm the glaze will melt away), dip a spoon into the glaze and use the back of the spoon to spread glaze over each cookie. Immediately sprinkle with crushed peppermint.

Lisa Worthey Smith

Packing Away Jesus, page 121

Chocolate Chip Bar (Deployment) Cookies

2 ¾ cups sifted AP flour

2 ½ tsp. baking powder

½ tsp. salt

1 cup chocolate morsels

    (or ½ chocolate and ½ butterscotch)

2/3 cup salted butter

    (1 stick =2 ½ Tbl.) melted

1 lb. light brown sugar

3 eggs

1 Tbl. vanilla extract (if you use imitation vanilla, use 2 Tbl.)

1 Tbl. butter flavoring

1 cup pecans, coarsely chopped

½ cup powdered sugar

Preheat oven to 350°

Grease 11" x 15" pan

    Mix and sift together flour, baking powder, and salt. Set aside.

    In a separate bowl, measure sugar, and pour melted butter over it. Stir well. Stir in flour mixture. Add eggs, beating after each one. Stir in morsels, pecans, vanilla, and butter flavoring.

    Spread batter into pan and **bake 20-30 minutes** until center rises and falls, top is golden brown, and edges pull away from the pan.

Note, the center may wiggle slightly, but will continue to cook after it comes out of the oven. As long the center reaches 125° (insert a cooking thermometer) the eggs will be done and you will keep the chewy center texture. If you judge by inserting a toothpick to the center it should come out nearly clean. If you wait until the toothpick is clean, they will probably be dry.

Cool in pan. Dust with powdered sugar (hint-dump into mesh strainer and shake over top or use Parmesan cheese shaker). Cut into 48 (2") squares.

To prepare for mailing

When completely cool, pour 1 Tbl. vanilla extract and 1 Tbl. butter flavoring in small bowl. Using a basting brush or a dropper, sprinkle over top of cookies.

After the flavorings have soaked in, dust with powdered sugar. Cut into squares. Wrap with aluminum foil and seal by folding edge-over-edge. Then insert into zipper style freezer bag. Squeeze out as much air as possible, then insert it into another zipper-style freezer bag.

When I mailed these overseas, they were enroute a week to ten days and survived well. Keep in mind the cool temperature in the winter will help. Summer mailing might have an undesirable result.

Lisa Worthey Smith

Faith in the Unknown, page 97

Creche Cookies

1 cup softened butter

1 cup brown sugar

1 cup white sugar

2 large eggs at room temperature

1 tsp. vanilla flavoring

2 cups all-purpose flour

1 tsp. salt

1 tsp. baking soda

3 cups old-fashioned oatmeal

1 cup shredded sweetened coconut

Candied pineapple wedges

Candied red cherry halves

Candied orange or lemon peel strips

Preheat oven to 350°

In a medium bowl, cream butter and sugars. Add vanilla flavoring and eggs. Combine well.

In a large bowl, sift flour, salt, and soda together. Stir in oatmeal and coconut.

Add creamed mixture to dry ingredients. Combine well.

Arrange paper cupcake liners on a baking sheet. Lightly spray inside each liner with butter-flavored cooking spray.

Fill each liner about 2/3 full of cookie dough.

Place a candied pineapple wedge on each mound of cookie dough. Place a candied cherry half, rounded side up, touching the narrow end of the pineapple wedge. Place a candied lemon peel strip (cut to slightly longer than the width of the cherry half) across the upper portion of the cherry half.

Bake at 350° for 14 to 18 minutes. Allow cookies to cool on the baking sheet 3 to 5 minutes before removing to a cooling rack.

Store between layers of wax paper in a sealed container.

Yields about 3 dozen large cookies.

Suzanne D. Nichols

My Messiah, page 29

The candied fruit arranged in the instructed manner resemble the Christ-child in swaddling clothes (complete with halo). The rustic cookie beneath resembles His hay-lined manger-bed.

Crescent Cookies

2/3 cup blanched almonds, whole

½ cup unsalted butter, softened

½ cup margarine, softened

1/3 cup sugar

1 2/3 cups all-purpose flour

¼ tsp. salt

Topping

½ cup sugar

½ tsp. cinnamon

Oven temperature 325°

Place almonds, half at a time, in a blender. Blend until finely chopped and set aside.

In a large bowl, combine butter, margarine, sugar and almonds. Blend with mixer on medium speed until light and fluffy. Sift the flour and salt together. Beat with the other mixture. Refrigerate the dough about 2 hours.

Cut the dough into 8 pieces. Flour your hands and form into 2 1/2 x1/2 inch ropes. Form crescent shapes. Place on ungreased cookie sheet and **bake for 12 – 14 minutes**.

Cool for 10 minutes. Roll in the topping.

Yield 4 dozen

June Foster

The Aroma of Christmas, page 57

June's Gingerbread Cookies

¾ cup unsalted butter softened

1 cup granulated sugar

1 large egg

¼ cup maple syrup

2 ½ cups all-purpose flour

2 tsp. baking soda

½ tsp. salt

2 tsp. cinnamon

½ tsp. ginger

Preheat oven to 350⁰.

Mix together butter and sugar until light and fluffy, approximately 2-3 minutes with an electric mixer.

Add egg and syrup.

In a separate bowl, combine flour, baking soda, salt, cinnamon and ginger, stirring to combine.

Add dry ingredients to wet ingredients and mix until well combined.

Form or scoop balls of dough that are slightly smaller than a golf ball. Place them on an ungreased baking sheet approximately 2"-3" apart to allow room for cookies to spread.

Bake for 10-12 minutes, remove from oven and allow cookies to cool on baking sheet for approximately ten minutes, then transfer to a wire rack to finish cooling.

Using an egg wash made with egg whites and a splash of water, brush cookies and add sprinkles of your choice of color.

Yields approximately a dozen cookies.

June Foster

Two Christmas Ornaments, page 37

Lemon Cherry Cookies

½ cup butter or margarine

½ cup sugar

1 egg separated

1 tsp. grated lemon peel

1 Tbl. lemon juice

1 cup all-purpose flour

½ cup finely chopped pecans

24 candied red cherries

Oven temperature 325°

With an electric mixer at medium speed, cream the butter and sugar until light and fluffy. Add egg yolk, lemon peel, and juice and beat until well blended. Gradually add flour and beat until well mixed.

Wrap dough in wax paper and chill for a least three hours or overnight.

Divide dough into quarters. Divide each quarter into 6 pieces and roll each piece into balls. Dip each in slightly beaten egg white and then into nuts.

Place on ungreased cookie sheets. Insert a cherry into the center of each.

Bake for 15 minutes. Cool.

Yields 24 cookies.

June Foster

The Fruit of the Spirit at Christmas Time, page 77

Lynn's Christmas Molasses Crinkles

¾ cup shortening

1 cup brown sugar

1 egg

4 Tbsp. molasses

4 tsp. salt

21/4 cups flour

2 tsp. baking soda

½ tsp. cloves

1 tsp. ginger

1 tsp. cinnamon

Preheat oven to 350°.

Lightly grease a cookie sheet.

Cream together sugar and shortening.

Beat egg and add molasses. Blend this with the creamed sugar and shortening.

Sift flour if needed and add to mixture.

Add remaining ingredients and blend together.

Chill dough in the refrigerator 1 hour or more.

Spoon out batter into your hand and roll into balls. Dip tops in sugar.

Place on the lightly greased cookie sheet.

Bake for 8 to 10 minutes.

Makes a dozen cookies.

Bonita Y. McCoy

The Branch, page 85

Maude's Molasses Cookies

2 cups all-purpose flour

2 tsp. baking soda

½ tsp. salt

1 ¾ tsp. ground cinnamon

1 tsp. ground cloves

1 tsp. ground ginger

¾ cup butter (room temperature)

1 cup white sugar

1 egg (room temperature and beaten)

¼ cup molasses (room temperature)

⅓ cup red or green decorating sugar

Preheat oven to 375°

Lightly grease baking sheet.

In small bowl, whisk together flour, baking soda, salt, cinnamon, cloves, and ginger. Set aside.

In medium bowl, use mixer on low speed to blend butter, white sugar, and egg until smooth. Mix in molasses. Gradually add flour mixture.

Cover and refrigerate dough for 1 hour.

Place decorating sugar in a small bowl.

Make 1-inch dough balls, and roll in decorating sugar.

144

Place them 2 inches apart on lightly greased cookie sheet. Flatten slightly with fork.

Bake for 8-10 minutes at 375° or just until tops are cracked all over and center is still gooey.

Makes approximately 2 dozen cookies.

Becky Alexander

A Familiar Ho Ho Ho, page 89

Merry Tea Cakes

For cookie dough:

1 cup butter (room temperature)

2 eggs (beaten)

2 cups sugar

2 tsp. vanilla

Approximately 4-5 cups flour

For icing:

1 lb. powdered sugar

½ cup butter (room temperature)

1 tsp. vanilla

3 Tbl. milk

Food coloring (your choice)

Preheat oven to 375°

In mixer, combine butter, eggs, sugar, and vanilla. Gradually add flour until right consistency to roll out.

Roll out dough and use cookie cutters dipped in flour to cut out your favorite Christmas shapes.

Place them 2 inches apart on lightly greased cookie sheet.

Bake for 7-9 minutes at 375° until slightly golden. Let cool.

Mix icing ingredients and spread on cookies.

Makes approximately 3 dozen cookies.

Becky Alexander

The Dreaded Family Christmas Celebration, page 69

These tea cakes are guaranteed to make your family merry!

Mother's Tea Cakes

1 cup butter

2 cups sugar

3 large eggs

2 tsp. vanilla flavoring

4 cups all-purpose flour

1 tsp. baking soda

Preheat oven to 350°

Allow butter and eggs to come to room temperature.

In a large bowl, cream butter and sugar. Add eggs one at a time, mixing after each addition. Add vanilla flavoring.

Combine flour and baking soda. Stir dry ingredients into creamed mixture a little at a time. Combine until a soft dough forms. Turn dough out onto a sheet of parchment dusted with flour.

Using a rolling pin lightly dusted with flour, roll dough out to a thickness of about ¼ inch.

Using a biscuit cutter lightly dusted with flour, cut dough into rounds. Place the cookies about two inches apart on a lightly greased baking sheet.

Bake at 350°, 8 to 10 minutes, or until lightly golden in color. Allow cookies to cool slightly before removing to a cooling rack.

Store between layers of wax paper in a sealed container.

Yields about 6 dozen tea cakes.

Suzanne D. Nichols

Welcoming the Light to My Christmas Table, page 93

Mother always arrived with a tin full of tea cakes for our Christmas reunions.

Nana's Christmas Cookies

1 cup oleo

2 eggs

1cup sugar

1 tsp. vanilla

1 tsp. cinnamon

2-1/2 cups flour

½ tsp. almond extract

½ cup finely chopped or ground pecans (as fine as powder)

Christmas cookie cutters

Pam or cooking spray

Preheat oven to 300° degrees.

Cream oleo and sugar together. Add eggs, cinnamon, vanilla extract, almond extract, and ground pecans. Mix well distributing the pecans throughout the dough. Add all the flour and mix again.

Turn the dough out onto wax paper and seal in plastic wrap. Chill for one to two hours in the refrigerator.

Flour board, rolling pin, and hands.

Take a small portion of the dough out of the bowl and return the rest to the refrigerator to stay cold.

Take as much flour as needed and work it into the dough with your hands. Add more flour until the dough isn't too sticky. Roll the dough out thin and use cookie cutters lightly sprayed with cooking oil to make the Christmas shapes. Decorate to your liking.

Bake for about 10 minutes. Cool, then store in a tightly sealed container, or do what we do and eat a few.

Yields 6 dozen (7 dozen when rolled thin).

Bonita Y. McCoy

The Star of Bethlehem, page 45

Sadie Snaps

1 box yellow or white cake mix

2 eggs (beaten)

5 Tbl. melted butter

2 cups mint chocolate chips

½ cup pecans (chopped)

Preheat oven to 350°

Mix ingredients.

Spread in a greased 9x13-inch pan.

Bake for 20 minutes at 350°.

After cooling, cut into squares.

Becky Alexander

Christmas Negotiations, page 1

Silent Night Delights

1 8-oz. cream cheese block (room

temperature)

½ cup butter (room temperature)

1 egg (beaten)

1 box strawberry cake mix

¼ cup walnuts (chopped)

¼ cup sweetened coconut flakes

¼ cup powdered sugar

Preheat oven to 350°

In mixer, cream together cream cheese and butter until smooth. Mix in

egg.

With mixer on low, slowly add cake mix. The dough will be

thick. Add walnuts and coconut flakes.

Refrigerate dough for 1 hour or until not overly sticky.

Line cookie sheet with parchment paper.

Place powdered sugar in a small bowl.

Make 1-inch dough balls, and roll in powdered sugar.

Place them 2 inches apart on cookie sheet.

Bake for 10 minutes on 350° or until centers are set.

Becky Alexander

The Chapel on Christmas Lane, page 25

Thumbprint Cookies

1 cup butter, room temperature

⅓ cup sugar + ½ cup for rolling

⅓ cup light brown sugar, tightly packed

1 large egg yolk

¼ tsp. vanilla extract

¼ tsp. butter extract

¼ tsp. almond extract

2 ¼ cup all purpose flour

2 tsp. cornstarch

½ tsp. salt

⅓ (about) cup preserves (I used homemade strawberry fig)

Preheat oven to 375°

Using a heavy stand mixer, cream butter. Scrape down the sides of the bowl, add sugars, and beat, gradually increasing mixer speed to medium-high until ingredients are well-combined.

Add egg yolk and vanilla extract and beat well.

In a separate bowl, stir together flour, cornstarch, and salt.

With mixer on low speed, gradually add flour mixture to wet ingredients until completely combined. (Dough will be dry and crumbly. Scrape the sides and bottom of the bowl occasionally, or work the dough with your hands.)

Spoon out walnut-sized balls and roll in hands until dough is round and has no cracks or seams.

Roll in granulated sugar. Place on a plate or cookie sheet covered with wax paper. Press your thumb in the center of each cookie, creating an indention.

Transfer to freezer and chill for 30 minutes. After dough is chilled, transfer cookies to a parchment-lined cookie sheet, (I like airbake) about 2 inches apart.

Preheat oven to 375° and warm the preserves in microwave or pan. The jam should be easy to stir, not steaming hot.

Using a small spoon, fill each thumbprint with jam. **Bake cookies for 11 minutes** or until edges are a very light golden brown. Allow cookies to cool completely on baking sheet before eating.

Lisa Worthey Smith

Pretty Packages, page 13

Vikki's Old-Fashioned Snickerdoodles

½ cup unsalted butter, softened

½ cup shortening

1 ½ cup sugar

2 large eggs

2 tsp. vanilla flavoring

2 ¾ cups all-purpose flour

2 tsp. cream of tartar

1 tsp. baking soda

¼ tsp. salt

3 Tbsp. sugar mixed with 3 Tbsp. cinnamon

Preheat oven to 375°

Allow butter and eggs to reach room temperature.

Cream butter, shortening, and sugar together in a large bowl. Blend in eggs and vanilla.

In a separate bowl, combine flour, cream of tartar, soda, and salt. Sir into creamed mixture.

Shape into 1-inch balls. Roll balls in the sugar and cinnamon mixture to coat.

Place balls 2 inches apart on an ungreased cookie sheet.

Bake 8 to 10 minutes. Remove immediately from cookie sheet.

Yields about 4 dozen cookies.

Dough may be refrigerated.

Suzanne D. Nichols

Lingering in the Awe, page 113

Our neighbor Vikki loves to surprise us with plates of baked goodies. Her Old-fashioned Snickerdoodles are a household favorite, especially when they're straight from the oven.

Winter Marvels

5 cups blended oatmeal

(measure oatmeal first, then

   blend in blender to a fine powder)

2 cups butter

2 cups sugar

2 cups packed brown sugar

4 large eggs

2 tsp. vanilla

4 cups flour

1 tsp. salt

2 tsp. baking powder

2 tsp. baking soda

24 oz. white chocolate chips

1 8-oz. Hershey Milk Chocolate Bar (grated)

3 cups chopped nuts (your choice)

1 cup sweetened coconut flakes

Preheat oven to 375°

Cream the butter and both sugars. Add eggs and vanilla.

Mix together the flour, oatmeal, salt, baking powder, and baking soda. Stir into butter mixture. Add white chocolate chips, grated Hershey bar, nuts, and coconut flakes.

Roll into 1-inch balls, and place 2 inches apart on a cookie sheet. **Bake for 10 minutes** or until golden.

Becky Alexander
A Winter Marvel, page 117

About the Authors

Becky Alexander loves all things Christmas, so co-authoring this book with her North Alabama writer friends made her merry and bright. It's her second Christmas book; in 2020, she contributed to *Moments' Christmas Stories* (Grace Publishing).

As a devotional writer for Guideposts, Becky's work appears in *Pray a Word a Day*, *God's Comforting Ways*, *In the Arms of Angels*, and *When God Makes Lemonade*. Her story "Connected by Kindness" in *Chicken Soup for the Soul: Miracles & Divine Intervention* received first-place awards from Carolina Christian Writers Conference and Southern Christian Writers Conference.

Clover's Wildflower Field Trip is filled with scientific facts and vocabulary words that support STEM standards for kindergarten through second grade. Becky collaborated with her biologist brother and teacher sister to write the colorful book as part of The Biology Bucket Series. Now, she's working on *Clover and Critters in the Creek*.

Becky teaches for the International Guide Academy and leads tours to Washington, D.C., New York, Toronto, Niagara Falls, Charleston, Nashville, and other destinations. Before her travel adventures, she taught kids about Jesus for twenty-five years as a children's minister.

Connect with Becky:

Say hi to Becky or order a copy of *Clover's Wildflower Field Trip* at HappyChairBooks.com.

An award-winning author, *June Foster* is also a retired teacher with a BA in Education and a MA in counseling. She is the mother of two and grandmother of ten.

June began writing Christian romance in 2010. She penned her first novel on her Toshiba laptop as she and her husband traveled the US in their RV. Her adventures provide a rich source of information for her novels. She brags about visiting a location before it becomes the setting in her next book.

To date, June has written over twenty contemporary romance and romantic suspense novels and novellas. She loves to compose stories about characters who overcome the circumstances in their lives by the power of God and His Word. June uses her training in counseling and her Christian beliefs in creating characters who find freedom to live godly lives. She's published with Winged Publications.

Connect with June

Visit her website at www.junefoster.com to see a complete list of her books.

Bonita Y. McCoy hails from the Great State of Alabama where she lives on a five-acre farm with two dogs, two cows, two cats, and one husband who she's had for over thirty years.

Her background includes a degree in Journalism from Mississippi State University as well as ten years teaching high school literature and writing classes to some of the best students, ever. She also served for twelve years as the Research Paper Coordinator for Life Christian Academy.

Her publishing adventure started at the ripe old age of thirteen when she worked for two years as a staff reporter for her school newspaper. Her senior year she worked on the School Yearbook as Junior Section Editor and did ad layouts for The Gulfport Star, a local newspaper.

More recent adventures include publishing her cozy mystery series with Winged Publications and being a finalist in the Silver Falchion Awards at Killer Nashville.

She is a mother to three grown sons and a beautiful daughter-in-law, who joined the family from Japan.

She loves God, and she loves to write. Her articles, blog, and novels are an expression of both these passions.

On any given day, you can find her photographing flowers, reading a sweet romance or a cozy mystery, or chilling on her front porch swing.

She is an active member of both American Christian Fiction Writers and Word Weavers International.

Connect with Bonita

Drop her a line at bonitaymccoy@yahoo.com or sign up for her newsletter at www.bonitaymccoy.com

Suzanne Dodge Nichols grew up in Gulf Breeze, Florida where, during a high school Composition Class, she discovered the rewarding discipline of writing. Through the years, she has found creative expression in almost every genre of the printed word. She especially enjoys blending words and art in ways that can both delight and challenge the observer.

With more than 30 years of experience leading Bible Drill, Suzanne has shared her life-long faith in God's Word with the children and youth of her church. During those years, she created Learn*Love*Live—a comprehensive, three-cycle curriculum for leading 4th – 6th graders in Children's Bible Drill, and Bible Basics—a companion or stand-alone curriculum focused on arming younger children with a greater measure of Bible knowledge, Scripture searching skills and confidence in God's Word.

Suzanne is a charter member of Word Weavers International North Alabama Chapter. She is published in the *2021 Divine Moments Christmas Spirit* anthology (Grace Publishing) and in seven volumes of the *Short and Sweet* series (Grace Publishing), a contributor to *Day by Day: 40 Devotionals for Writers & Creative Types* (Southern Christian Writers Conference), and is a 2021 Selah Awards recipient.

Suzanne makes her home in Hartselle, Alabama with her husband of 45 years. They have three children and nine grandchildren who live *much* too far away.

 ***Ginger Solomon*** is a Christian, a wife, a mother to seven, and a writer—in that order (mostly).

She writes or reads inspirational romance of any genre. She also likes needlework—crocheting and knitting, mostly—and has discovered a love for acrylic painting.

She blogs regularly for InspyRomance.com and at gingersolomon.com.

Connect with Ginger

Website GingerSolomon.com

Blog InspyRomance.com

Twitter.com/@GingerS219

Pinterest.com/GingerS219

Amazon.com Ginger Solomon (Author Page)

Lisa Worthey Smith is a long-time Bible student and in-depth Bible study leader, with a passion to point people to the Word of God. Serving as president of Word Weavers North Alabama, this multiple award-winning author coaches and prays over a number of writers, helping them pursue their God-given talents and writing missions.

Called to encourage, edify, and educate, Lisa publishes through Kerysso Press. Based on the Greek word κηρύσσω, "kerysso" means to herald, especially divine truth. Kerysso was used of the public proclamation of the gospel and matters pertaining to it, made by John the Baptist, by Jesus, by the apostles, and other Christian teachers.

Lisa and her high-school sweetheart husband are empty-nesting in north Alabama where she writes with a cup of Earl Grey beside her.

Connect with Lisa
Twitter.com@LisaWSmith57
Instagram.com/@LisaW.Smith
Pinterest.com/Lisa Worthey Smith
Mewe.com/LisaSmith1552
Find all her books under her Amazon author page, Lisa Worthey Smith

Made in the USA
Middletown, DE
22 March 2023

26819601R00109